THE REVELATION OF JESUS CHRIST

The End Times

Tiffany Root & Kirk VandeGuchte

Seeking the Glory of God Ministries

The Revelation of Jesus Christ

The End Times

Edited, formatted, and published by

Destiny House Publishing, LLC.

P.O. Box 19774

Detroit, MI 48219

inquiry@destinyhousepublishing.com

www.destinyhousepublishing.com

404.993.0830

Cover by Kingdom Graphic Designs

Printed in the United States

ISBN: 978-1-936867-89-9

TABLE OF CONTENTS

Introduction.. 1

Chapter 1: What is Revelation? 3

Chapter 2: Eschatology – What is it & how to choose the right one 10

Chapter 3: What About a Rapture? 22

Chapter 4: Tribulation & Persecution 38

Chapter 5: Jesus' End Times Teachings........................ 49

Chapter 6: The Book of Revelation – the Beginning 64

Chapter 7: The Seven Seals & the Seven Trumpets 73

Chapter 8: Revelation Chapters 12, 13, & 14............................. 87

Chapter 9: The Bowls of Wrath 97

Chapter 10: The End of the Babylon World System 109

Chapter 11: The Two Witnesses................................. 116

Chapter 12: The Millennial Reign & the New Jerusalem 122

Chapter 13: Can God Use Prophecies More Than Once? 136

INTRODUCTION

On August 20, 2021, the Holy Spirit told me (Tiffany) that He wanted to give me revelation into the book of Revelation and into the end times. The following is what He said.

"Apostles see the big picture and bring it back to Jesus. Remember, Jesus is what I'm interested in talking about."

He then asks me, *"What do you see in Revelation?"*

I answered, "I see the world system collapsing (Babylon has fallen), and I see judgments come on the earth, but Your people standing and free. I see Revelation is not written linearly, but prophetically, as Kirk has seen. I see the beast and the dragon are nothing. All they have are lies. I see the saints – the real remnant – like the two apostles or the little girl in Joyner's vision (*The Final Quest Series*). They are battle hardened, filled with love and joy, having been tested and coming through. I see Kirk's word about how You've placed us all in a certain situation at a certain time and we must do our part for the good of others. So yes, some are experiencing beheading, mutilation, terrible torture, death, imprisonment, and starvation. Some are in a position to fight for and support those who are so treated. All are doing their part following the Holy Spirit. I see we pay too much attention to what is fading away and not enough to what will last forever. I see love conquers all darkness, and Jesus has already won. When we choose Jesus, we choose victory."

The Lord says, *"You have seen correctly. What I Am about to show you then, you will put with the big picture and teach others also how to live by revelation, what it means, and who it comes through. Revelation is called the Revelation of Jesus Christ for it is the story of the history of mankind and the God who became a Man to save him."*

The following is what He showed us. Enjoy!

CHAPTER 1

WHAT IS REVELATION?

————————◆◄◄◆►►◆————————

Merriam-Webster's dictionary defines revelation as the act of revealing or communicating divine truth or the act of revealing or making known.

Peter received revelation of Jesus Christ in Matthew 16:13-18.

> When Jesus came into the region of Caesarea Philippi, He asked His disciples, saying, "Who do men say that I, the Son of Man, am?" So they said, "Some say John the Baptist, some Elijah, and others Jeremiah or one of the prophets." He said to them, "But who do you say that I am?" Simon Peter answered and said, "You are the Christ, the Son of the living God." Jesus answered and said to him, "Blessed are you, Simon Bar-Jonah, for flesh and blood has not revealed this to you, but My Father who is in heaven. And I also say to you that you are Peter, and on this rock I will build My church, and the gates of Hades shall not prevail against it."

Father revealed to Peter that Jesus was the Messiah, and Jesus said the revelation of Jesus Christ is what the church is built upon. When we receive a revelation from God, it will be something about Jesus because Jesus is the revelation of the Father to us (Hebrews 1:1-4). Everything points to Jesus and originates from Him. As Colossians 1:15-17 states:

> He is the image of the invisible God, the firstborn over all creation. For by Him all things were created: things in heaven and on earth, visible and invisible, whether thrones or powers or rulers or

authorities; all things were created by Him and for Him. He is before all things, and in Him all things hold together. (NIV)

In other words, everything is all about Jesus. All revelation from God is about Him – the One who reveals Father to us. And yet, some think that we do not need any more revelation because we have the Scriptures. Let's look at a couple of passages to see if that is true.

But Peter, standing up with the eleven, raised his voice and said to them, "Men of Judea and all who dwell in Jerusalem, let this be known to you, and heed my words. For these are not drunk, as you suppose, since it is only the third hour of the day. But this is what was spoken by the prophet Joel:

'And it shall come to pass afterward
That I will pour out My Spirit on all flesh;
Your sons and your daughters shall prophesy,
Your old men shall dream dreams,
Your young men shall see visions.
And also on My menservants and My maidservants
I will pour out My Spirit in those days;
And they shall prophesy.
I will show wonders in heaven above
And signs in the earth beneath:
Blood and fire and vapor of smoke.
The sun shall be turned into darkness
And the moon into blood,
Before the coming of the great and awesome day of the LORD.
And it shall come to pass
That whoever calls on the name of the LORD
Shall be saved." (Acts 2:14-21)

Do you think those who read the book of Joel before the Holy Spirit was poured out had any idea what was going to happen? If they had known, do you think they would have chastised the disciples and called them "drunk"?

Peter revealed what the passage in Joel meant to those who watched what happened on Pentecost. The meaning of the Scripture was revealed to show that Jesus had poured out His Spirit on mankind.

This is why we need revelation. Without revelation, we can read the entire Bible and not understand what God is saying. It's not enough to just have the Scriptures. We have to have the Holy Spirit revealing the truth to us through those Scriptures. And remember, Jesus is the Truth, so the revelation we receive will point to Him, and it will come through His Spirit. If revelation is truth that God reveals to us, and the Holy Spirit is the Spirit of Truth who leads us into all truth, is there any other way to arrive at the truth than by the Holy Spirit? He is, after all, the One who knows the deep things of God.

Jesus testifies that all things the Father has are His (John 16:13-15). These are the things He gives to the Holy Spirit to speak to us. These are the mysteries of God. And these mysteries are given to us by the Holy Spirit. There's no other way to receive revelation than by the Holy Spirit.

But what about if an angel of the Lord brings us revelation? For example, one of the angels brought the interpretation of a vision to Daniel, which was a revelation of his vision. Is that by the Holy Spirit too? Of course it is. The angels of God are empowered by the Holy Spirit, and we receive the revelations they bring us by the Holy Spirit.

What if Jesus Himself appears to us? Can we receive revelation from Christ Himself, and then that wouldn't be by the Holy Spirit? The Father asks, *"Can you do something apart from the Spirit within you?"* Of course not. We receive these revelations through the Spirit of

Christ. Jesus poured out His Spirit on us that we may know Him by His Spirit, and Jesus is the revelation of the Father.

When we receive revelation from Jesus Christ through His Spirit, it will line up with Scripture. However, it will not always line up with our understanding of Scripture. This is because before the Holy Spirit reveals something to us, we only have intellectual knowledge to go on. Intellectual knowledge is not revelation. Revelation of Jesus Christ is a firm foundation that cannot be shaken. Intellectual knowledge of Scripture is shaky, at best. It will not hold up in a storm.

Therefore, be willing to allow the Holy Spirit to give you revelation and show you in the Scriptures how the revelation is true. When you do this, you are saying you give up your intellectual understanding of the Scriptures in favor of what He reveals them to actually mean.

In Matthew 9:9-13, Jesus took a portion of Scripture to explain what He was doing when He ate with tax collectors and sinners. The Pharisees knew the Scriptures, but the revelation Jesus gave didn't line up with their interpretation of the Scriptures. They had a choice to make – either believe their interpretation or believe Jesus. If they believed their interpretation, they couldn't accept what Jesus said. If they believed Jesus, they had to change the way they interpreted the Scriptures.

It's important that we remember that Jesus is the Truth. The Holy Spirit of Christ leads us into all Truth. The Scriptures will bear witness to that truth because they testify of Jesus Christ. If we can keep this in the forefront, it will help us tremendously when we receive revelation.

Do Scriptures lead you into all truth, or does the Holy Spirit? The Scriptures themselves testify that revelation does not come because we study Scripture and understand something with our intellect

(John 5:39). Revelation comes because we surrender to the Holy Spirit, who leads us into all truth. He is the Spirit of Christ. He is the One who knows the deep things of God. He is the One who inspired the Scriptures. He will interpret what the Scriptures mean.

When the Holy Spirit brings us a revelation and it doesn't line up with our understanding of a portion of Scripture, then we re-evaluate that Scripture with the Holy Spirit. We allow Him to interpret the Scriptures and tell us what they mean, instead of us deciding what something means and making sure that whatever we hear lines up with our interpretation.

In some way all revelation will reveal Jesus. As it does, it lifts Him up. The Scriptures say that we shall all be taught by God. His Spirit searches the deep things of God and reveals them to us in our spirits. These deep things of God are revelation of God, or we could say, they are revelation of Jesus Christ. He has come to us as the revelation of our Father. If you are hearing something presented as revelation that does not lift up Jesus, it is not real revelation.

For example, many teachings about the end times lift up the antichrist and lift up evil to such an extreme that it is taught that the times will be so bad God will have to rescue His church out of them because they won't be able to handle it. That kind of teaching does not lift up Jesus. Jesus took the keys of death and Hades from the enemy and gave all authority and power to His church. He's coming back for a victorious, pure bride, who is like Him.

Additionally, revelation will not aggrandize the individual who brings it. (Aggrandize means to make greater or appear greater.) Everything we have we've received from God. This includes revelation. So, if we receive revelation, it has come from the Lord, and will bring glory to Him. This doesn't mean people won't be impressed with the revelation we receive, just as they may be impressed with gifts of the Holy Spirit, like prophecy or healing, etc. When you walk in spiritual gifts, you can't help how others respond, but the gifts will exalt Jesus, regardless of how others view you.

It's the same with revelation. You can't help it if you bring revelation and people start to exalt you. You can try to get them stop, just as Paul and Barnabas tried to get the people in Lystra to refrain from sacrificing to them when they healed someone (Acts 14:8-18). Paul and Barnabas were successful, and then the people turned on them and stoned Paul, leaving him for dead. It just goes to show how we cannot put our trust in the opinions of men.

In like manner, the response of others isn't up to you. However, when you receive revelation or hear it from someone else, it will lift up Jesus. All revelation lifts up Jesus.

Most of the revelation you receive outside of personal revelation will come through the apostles because the apostles are tasked with bringing revelation to the church. It is the Holy Spirit who leads us into all truth, including revelation. And it is by the Holy Spirit that the apostles revelated in Scripture. The same is true today. Apostles receive revelation by the Holy Spirit.

As they revelate, Apostles will not be lifting up a book but lifting up Jesus. When you worship a book, every verse holds the same weight. When you worship the Lord, then there's a distinction. Some verses carry more weight than others. It's all based on what the Holy Spirit reveals about Jesus, and it's the apostles who are tasked with bringing the revelation of Jesus to the Church.

As we go into the Revelation of Jesus Christ and the end times, we need to remember that our opinions do not count, much study does not count, degrees and doctorates do not count. It is only the revelation of Jesus that really matters. The Holy Spirit will bear witness to true revelation because He witnesses of Jesus. Therefore, ask Him to read this book with you and to lead you into all truth.

CHAPTER 2

ESCHATOLOGY – WHAT IT IS & HOW TO CHOOSE THE RIGHT ONE

—————————◆ ◆◆ ◆ ◆◆ ◆—————————

Eschatology is the study of the end times. It is the word used when someone defines what they believe will happen at the end of time, the end of the world, the end of humankind, or the end of the age, etc. In a basic sense, eschatology is someone's belief of the end times. There are many different beliefs regarding what will happen at the end of time, even in Christianity, let alone combined with other religions.

Your view of how things will end up will determine how you live now. If you believe nothing you do is going to make a difference, and the world's going to burn up in short order, you would likely live life fast and loose for great pleasure now. Because, hey – it's not going to matter anyway! You wouldn't need to pick up after yourself, look to make anything better on any long-term scale, really consider how your choices affect others, or make choices that would affect your life later. It's live for today, and don't worry about tomorrow.

If you believe things are going to get better in the world, that the world will endure for a long time, and that you can make a difference, you may look for ways to make an impact on the world around you. You may pray for creativity and skill so that you can be a part of making the world a better place. You would care about the people and the world around you because you would understand it's going to be here long after you're gone. Your decisions would not be short-sighted, but long-sighted.

To take it even further, if your eschatology included an afterlife, you would make decisions based on an eternal future, not just a temporary one. You would consider how your decisions might affect you and others in eternity. For a Christian, this means you would be concerned about the eternal welfare of others. If you had a view of either living eternally or dying eternally, it would impact how you interacted with others because you would understand that life is more than just what we see physically on earth. You would know that the choices we make in this world affect what happens to us in the next world.

Our actions are determined by what we believe.

> **What does it profit, my brethren, if someone says he has faith but does not have works? Can faith save him? If a brother or sister is naked and destitute of daily food, and one of you says to them, "Depart in peace, be warmed and filled," but you do not give them the things which are needed for the body, what does it profit? Thus also faith by itself, if it does not have works, is dead. (James 2:14-17)**

James said that faith without works is dead, meaning if you truly believe something, you will act on it. People who truly believe in freedom, fight for it. People who truly believe abortion is evil, work and pray to end it. People who truly believe Jesus is Lord, follow Him. People who truly believe God is love, love others. People who truly believe God is a rewarder, diligently seek Him. The list could go on and on. What you truly believe affects how you act.

Therefore, it's important to have God's view of the end times. Your belief in what God clearly reveals through the revelation of His Son will impact how you live in these end times.

So how do we choose the right eschatology to believe?

Jesus said that we live on every word that comes forth from the mouth of God, and Paul testified that all wisdom and knowledge is hidden in Christ (Matthew 4:4, Colossians 2:3). Therefore, we get the right view of the end times by revelation of Jesus Christ. That's the only way. It's time for the church to start living by revelation, instead of by the intellect. (Galatians 1:11-12)

Logic and reason are a good option to following the Holy Spirit, which is why many people choose it. The intellect seems pretty good. And it is. Through your intellect, you can reason and deduce things and come to logical conclusions. You can weigh differing arguments and opinions. You can determine which argument or opinion has the most Scripture to back it up. You can decide what is right or what is wrong based on your intellect. Therefore, in considering your eschatology, you can formulate just what you think is right based on reasoning. You can do this. And you can be completely wrong.

Paul said that he received the gospel that he preached through revelation of Jesus Christ. Revelation is so much higher than the intellect, it's really not even comparable. Revelation may not make sense to the intellect at first, but it will be proved right in the end. And with all revelation, Jesus will be the focus. He is the revelation of the Father given to us. He must be the focus. He's who Father is interested in talking about.

Have you ever noticed that most people have a view of the end times that is almost solely focused on the devil and how bad things will be? The book of Revelation is the Revelation of Jesus Christ, not the revelation of the devil. Focusing on bad causes people to take their eyes off Jesus, and in doing so, kills faith. Jesus is the author and perfector of our faith. How are you going to be filled with faith if your eyes are on the enemy, how big and bad he is, and what the enemy is doing and is going to do? Jesus has to be the focus of your end times theology, and He will be if your eschatology is revelation instead of logic or reason.

Revelation for the church comes through the apostles. Those apostles who preach only by revelation can be trusted to bring to you the truth about the end times. Those apostles who have been trained by the Lord to live by revelation, will teach others to do the same. Your spirit will recognize when something preached to you is revelation of Jesus Christ. The Holy Spirit bears witness with your spirit that what you are hearing is the truth. **"Then you will know the truth, and the truth will set you free"** – Jesus. (John 8:32, NIV)

In order to receive revelation you first need to be filled with the Holy Spirit so that you can understand the deep things of God, you need to be willing to lay down what you've been taught and what you believe so that your heart can be open to what the Holy Spirit brings you regarding the end times, and you have to give up your right to understand. Faith first believes and allows understanding to come later. What Holy Spirit brings will be revelation, and as such, it will lift up Jesus.

Now, regarding all of the end time details, we must keep in mind that Jesus tells us what is happening and the Scriptures back Him up as a witness. It's not the other way around. So, we don't figure something out from Scripture with our intellect and then try to hear something from God to back it up. The Holy Spirit leads us into all truth and the Scriptures testify of that truth.

Unfortunately, most "Christians" do not really understand what it means to be a disciple of Jesus Christ. They still think they have the "right" to have opinions. But when Jesus called His followers "disciples," He showed by example that a disciple is one who lays down their life for their Master (Luke 9:23-25). This doesn't just mean a disciple should be willing to die physically for Jesus. This means a disciple lays down what they think, who they used to be, what they want, and instead they follow Jesus. They choose to listen to and obey His Spirit. They choose to believe what He says is truth instead of what they think is truth. They choose to give up what they want, for what He says.

The desire to live for self plays into some Christians' theologies, especially their eschatology. Once someone has decided that they are right about something, it takes a lot of humility to change their mind and decide they are wrong. If a Christian hasn't learned to die to self as a disciple of Jesus, changing their mind on what they believe is really scary.

When you formulate an opinion, you have to defend it. Whereas if you live by revelation, you are convinced in your heart of what God has revealed to you, and what other people believe doesn't cause you to become defensive and angry. If you're questioned on your beliefs, you are able to explain what you believe, without the need to convince someone else. You trust the Holy Spirit to do the work in their heart, and you just speak what He gives you to say in the moment.

Living by revelation means the truth is in your heart, and your trust is in Jesus. This isn't just something you say, but something that you live. When you have opinions, you are not trusting in Jesus. Instead, you trust that your intellect has brought you to the right conclusions, and consequently, you must depend on self to defend your views. It's pretty stressful. And it causes you to shut down others that do not believe the same way that you do.

Pride always rejects the notion that it could be wrong. Humility agrees with God. If you've tried discussing eschatology with people who are defensive and unwilling to discuss it, they have an idol in the way of Jesus. They have built upon a faulty foundation based on intellect, and it will be painful for them to tear it down. They've lifted up something they believe higher than the Truth Himself. They will need to repent in order to see the truth. You can pray *for* them, but it's unlikely they'll let you pray *with* them, because then they would have to admit they may need help, and who needs help if you have it all right?

As you discuss the end times with people, steer clear of opinions, and just seek the Lord for revelation. You will avoid a lot of needless arguing and grief if your goal is the truth that is in Jesus.

When we have a stronghold about something, we tend to interpret Scripture according to our stronghold. It's like having cataracts on our eyes. They change our view of things. John 12:34 says, **"The people answered Him, "We have heard from the law that the Christ remains forever; and how can You say, 'The Son of Man must be lifted up'? Who is this Son of Man?"** Because Jesus wasn't doing things the way they interpreted Scripture, the people thought He couldn't be the Messiah. However, they interpreted Scripture wrong. In a similar manner, if you have been taught that the Church must escape tribulation, you will read Scripture with that mindset and have a difficult time seeing that you will not escape tribulation. Jesus says about the church in Smyrna in Revelation 2:9a, **"I know your works, tribulation…"**. These people were already going through tribulation, and it hasn't stopped happening to believers still today.

We need to seek the Lord before we accept something as truth. Ask the Lord to show you truth about the rapture, the tribulation, and the end times. Be willing to lay down what you believe. He will show you if you sincerely want to know. Be patient. Just because you lay something down doesn't mean you're wrong, but you might be, and you need to be willing to be wrong in order to know truth. Jesus is Truth and He leads us in all truth by His Holy Spirit whom He has given us.

Paul writes in 1 Thessalonians 3:4, **"For, in fact, we told you before when we were with you that we would suffer tribulation, just as it happened, and you know."** Paul and his companions suffered tribulation. Believers all over the world suffer tribulation. It happens all the time. We are promised persecution for following Jesus. It's nothing of which to be afraid. We are glorified as we suffer with Him, the Bible says (Romans 8:17). Jesus wasn't raptured out of His suffering, and we will not be either.

Our faith and love must be tested, and it is often tested through suffering. Will we keep believing and will we keep loving amidst suffering? Anything of value is tested, and tribulations and trials help to do that for us.

The baseline for end times theology should be what Jesus clearly said because what Jesus says holds the most sway. So, when Jesus gives us parables to explain what the end times will be like, we need to make sure that what He says is our baseline of belief. In the Parable of the Wheat and Tares, Jesus explains to us what the Kingdom of Heaven is like and what will happen during the end times.

> Another parable He put forth to them, saying: "The Kingdom of heaven is like a man who sowed good seed in his field; but while men slept, his enemy came and sowed tares among the wheat and went his way. But when the grain had sprouted and produced a crop, then the tares also appeared. So the servants of the owner came and said to him, 'Sir, did you not sow good seed in your field? How then does it have tares?' He said to them, 'An enemy has done this.' The servants said to him, 'Do you want us then to go and gather them up?' But he said, 'No, lest while you gather up the tares you also uproot the wheat with them. Let both grow together until the harvest, and at the time of harvest I will say to the reapers, 'First gather together the tares and bind them in

bundles to burn them, but gather the wheat into my barn.'" (Matthew 13:24-30)

Then Jesus sent the multitude away and went into the house. And His disciples came to Him, saying, "Explain to us the parable of the tares of the field." He answered and said to them: "He who sows the good seed is the Son of Man. The field is the world, the good seeds are the sons of the kingdom, but the tares are the sons of the wicked one. The enemy who sowed them is the devil, the harvest is the end of the age, and the reapers are the angels. Therefore as the tares are gathered and burned in the fire, so it will be at the end of this age. The Son of Man will send out His angels, and they will gather out of His kingdom all things that offend, and those who practice lawlessness, and will cast them into the furnace of fire. There will be wailing and gnashing of teeth. Then the righteous will shine forth as the sun in the kingdom of their Father. He who has ears to hear, let him hear!" (Matthew 13:36-43)

The Son of Man, who is Christ, sows only good seed. He cannot sow bad seed. He cannot do evil. He only does what He sees His Father doing. There's no evil in God. There's no evil in the Son. This means that those who are in Christ are good. They are the good seed that develops into the wheat. As wheat matures, it bows down because the head becomes heavy with grain. This is true of those who mature in Christ. They become more humble as they mature. They become more like their Master, who could do nothing of Himself, but only did what He saw His Father doing. When we die to ourselves and live for God, we agree with the LORD in everything. We give up opinions, lies, and selfish desires for His thoughts, the truth, and His ways. Mature wheat will bow. Mature sons will bow.

Conversely, tares will grow up with the wheat, looking very much like the wheat until the point of maturity happens. In this case, the tares will continue to stand up, while the wheat bows down. In Jesus' parable, the tares are the sons of the evil one. The sons of the devil will not bow to Jesus. They will not allow Jesus to be the head, and they are recognized for who they are as the wheat and tares mature together.

At this point, the angels come in and take out the tares. The tares are easy to spot because in their pride, they're standing tall. They're not ashamed of their wickedness, and they're looking for accolades from men as they stand proud in the wind. The angels are sent to take them out.

After the angels remove those who are sons of the devil, what will be left? The sons of God will shine in the kingdom of their Father. Without the sons of the devil, the sons of God, or the righteous, are the ones who are left.

This same truth is reiterated in the Parable of the Dragnet.

> **"Again, the kingdom of heaven is like a dragnet that was cast into the sea and gathered some of every kind, which, when it was full, they drew to shore; and they sat down and gathered the good into vessels, but threw the bad away. So it will be at the end of the age. The angels will come forth, separate the wicked from among the just, and cast them into the furnace of fire. There will be wailing and gnashing of teeth."** (Matthew 13:47-50)

Jesus again gives us a picture of what the Kingdom of Heaven is like. He says the sons of the evil one are like bad fish. Who wants to eat bad fish? No one. Just like in the Parable of the Wheat and Tares, the angels are sent to take the bad fish and throw them into the fire. The angels are literally removing the sons of the devil from the earth.

Those who remain are the good fish. We know these are the sons of God because no one is good except those found in Christ.

In each parable, Jesus shows us what the Kingdom of Heaven is like. The Kingdom does not have evil in it. The angels are tasked with removing evil when it matures. And the righteous are left to shine like the sun in the Kingdom of their Father. In other words, it looks like bad is removed, good is left, and righteousness prevails.

That is the baseline for end times theology. These are two comparable parables that Jesus taught to specifically show us what it would be like in the end times. If you look around you, you can see it happening even now.

Even though this is our baseline, Jesus made it very clear that no one would know the time of His return, not the angels in Heaven, or even the Son. That's interesting because we know that angels can see ahead to plan where to be to help us when we need it and so forth. But this particular event is hidden from them. We also know that Jesus has returned to the Father and is glorified, and yet the time of His return is hidden from Him as well.

> **"But of that day and hour no one knows, not even the angels of heaven, but My Father only. But as the days of Noah were, so also will the coming of the Son of Man be. For as in the days before the flood, they were eating and drinking, marrying and giving in marriage, until the day that Noah entered the ark, and did not know until the flood came and took them all away, so also will the coming of the Son of Man be. Then two men will be in the field; one will be taken and the other left. Two women will be grinding at the mill; one will be taken and the other left. Watch therefore, for you do not know what hour your Lord is coming. But know this, that if the master of the house had known what hour the thief would come, he would have watched and not allowed his house to**

19

be broken into. Therefore you also be ready, for the Son of Man is coming at an hour you do not expect." (Matthew 24:36-44)

So even though Jesus and the angels do not know when the end will be, men still keep trying to figure it out. They write books and sermons telling us we need to look for this particular event or that particular sign before Jesus will return. They do all of this figuring with their minds, even though we understand that we cannot know the things of God through our intellect. We can only know the things of God by the Spirit of God. Therefore, unless the Holy Spirit reveals something to us, we do not have understanding into that particular topic. And yet, men, even men who are highly exalted in the "church," believe they know how things will be. They believe they know what's going to happen and when.

They base all of this so-called knowledge on what they've figured out by piecing together Scriptures to make those Scriptures fit a desired outcome. But somehow they miss what Jesus said the end would be like. When we read the Scriptures, it's most important to pay attention to what Jesus said. He is the Word of God, and so what He spoke in Scripture carries the most weight. Jesus said it will be like in the days of Noah.

In the days of Noah, the people of the world had no idea what was coming. They went about their lives working, marrying, having birthday parties, going about their business **until the flood came and took them all away."** (Matthew 24:39) They didn't realize the wicked were being taken out of the earth. They didn't realize there was judgment coming, even though Noah had evidently been preaching righteousness as he built the ark (2 Peter 2:5). The wicked grew up right along with the righteous until they were taken out, and that's how it will be in the end, which can be clearly seen in Jesus' parable of the wheat and the tares. (Matthew 13:24-30, 36-43)

We can see the last days are upon us. We can see, according to Scripture and the current prophetic words given to the Prophets, that we are at the point where the wicked are taken out and the great harvest is beginning. Those who listen to the Holy Spirit and have eyes to see can believe this and see it. And yet, even though we can see this as revealed by the Holy Spirit, we do not know when the end will be.

Those who do not see and do not submit their intellect to the Holy Spirit will continue to use their intellect to try to figure something out, declaring a knowledge that they do not have. Jesus said no one would know when the end would come, and though we can see the things the Holy Spirit reveals to us, we do not claim to know when the end will come. Those who do are not telling you by revelation of Jesus Christ. They're telling you by a different spirit. Don't listen to them.

Jesus doesn't even know the time that the Father has reserved for Himself. We do not know either. What we do know is that it is going to be good for those who are in Christ.

CHAPTER 3

WHAT ABOUT A RAPTURE?

A ccording to The American Heritage Dictionary of the English Language, 5th Edition, "Rapture" means:

1.   The state of being transported by a lofty emotion; ecstasy.
2. An expression of ecstatic feeling.
3. The transporting of a person from one place to another, especially to heaven, by supernatural means.

When Christians refer to "the rapture" they are referring to the teaching that Jesus is going to take His church out of the earth at some point, and the only people left will be the unbelievers. There are so many different teachings regarding this, that it can be dizzying. One group argues for a rapture before what they like to term the "Great Tribulation." Others argue for a rapture during the "Great Tribulation." Still others argue for a rapture after a "Great Tribulation." Some people think the number of years given in Scripture are literal. Others think the number of years are figurative. Some people think Jesus' second coming and a rapture are one event. Some think the second coming is separate from the rapture, and the rapture happens first, making it two second comings.

All of this is very confusing and highly intellectual. There are scriptures that are used to defend each particular point of view with their own varying details. There are scholars to back up each view of the rapture. And there are books upon books written to try to answer all the questions brought up by this teaching. Because the rapture teaching contradicts so much of the Bible and what Jesus taught, and really who God is and how He operates, it requires these Bible scholars to basically jump through hoops to answer all the questions raised. I even came across one of these people's answer to the question: What happens to the Holy Spirit after the Church is raptured? The person said that the Holy Spirit is no longer needed at this point. What? Really? Clearly, they do not have an understanding of Jesus, the power of God, or the Scriptures. Jesus said He was giving us the Holy Spirit to be with us forever and that He would never leave us or forsake us. (John 14:16, Hebrews 13:5) Besides that, how are we holy if we don't have the Holy Spirit? Suddenly we'll get holy on our own effort in heaven?

The rapture teaching is demonic. It's not from the Holy Spirit. Jesus has given you the power through His Spirit to overcome all the power of the enemy, and Jesus is always with you through His Spirit whom He has given to you to abide in you forever. So where did the rapture teaching come from?

There are several people of whom it could be said that the rapture teaching started in the last several hundred years. There was a Baptist preacher named Morgan Edwards who preached a rapture in the 1700's. Possibly the most famous preacher of a rapture, and the one who really got the teaching going is John Darby, who started preaching a rapture in 1827. Then there was a woman named Margaret MacDonald who had a vision in 1830 that people say was a rapture vision. I have read the vision, and do not see a rapture in it. It seems to be a vision in which she is prophesying about the outpouring of the Holy Spirit and the lifting up of Jesus in the last days. It seems as though John Darby took her vision and made it "fit" what he was teaching to lead people astray. Regardless, she's credited with helping the rapture teaching gain momentum.

What we do not find as we look in history for where the rapture teaching began is Jesus teaching a rapture. He didn't teach one. The first apostles didn't teach a rapture, even though some of their writings are taken that way. And the apostles that came after the 12, like the Apostle Paul, did not teach a rapture.

Jesus and His apostles certainly taught that Jesus would come again in the same way that they saw Him leave, but they did not teach a rapture. In fact, if Jesus is saying that His people would see Him return in the same manner in which He left, it's a pretty obvious indication that His people will be on earth when He returns.

> **Now when He had spoken these things, while they watched, He was taken up, and a cloud received Him out of their sight. And while they looked steadfastly toward heaven as He went up, behold, two men stood by them in white apparel, who also said, "Men of Galilee, why do you stand gazing up into heaven? This same Jesus, who was taken up from you into heaven, will so come in like manner as you saw Him go into heaven." (Acts 1:9-11)**

In order to know whether or not the church will be raptured out of the world if things get too bad for them to handle, we have to know what the purpose of the church is.

Jesus told us several things, one of which was to go into all the world and make disciples of all the nations. (Matthew 28:19) If there were a rapture, we certainly couldn't leave before we had accomplished this task.

Another thing the Lord tasks His church with is to make known to the principalities and powers the manifold wisdom of God. (Ephesians 3:10) If the church is removed from the earth, we could no longer fulfill this calling.

His intent was that now, through the church, the manifold wisdom of God should be made known to the rulers and authorities in the heavenly realms, according to His eternal purpose which He accomplished in Christ Jesus our Lord. (Ephesians 3:10-11, NIV)

It is God's intent that the gospel is proclaimed through the church and that through the church the manifold wisdom of God is revealed to the powers of darkness. It is not His intent to take the church out of the way, because it's the church that brings the gospel to the world. The whole creation is groaning as it waits for the sons of God to be revealed. Why? Because those of us who are born again and filled with the Spirit of the LORD are commissioned to bring heaven to earth. Creation has been bound since the Fall of man and is waiting for freedom. (See Romans 8:19-23.)

We preach the gospel of the Kingdom with signs and wonders following in preparation for the return of the King. As we do, we establish Hs kingdom on earth.

The word "apostle" comes from Rome. In the days of the Roman kingdom, apostles were sent out to make conquered territories just like Rome so that when the Emperor came to visit, he would feel comfortable. He would feel like he was at home. Jesus too sends out apostles to make conquered territories like Heaven so that when He returns, He feels at home. The Church is directed to bring His kingdom to earth. Why then would Jesus come back and take the church away when His apostles lead the church to bring Heaven to earth for His return? It makes no sense at all. On the contrary, when Jesus returns, it is the wicked and those who offend who are taken away, not the righteous.

The apostles and prophets lay the foundation for the church because they bring the revelation of Jesus Christ to the church. As Paul writes,

> Now, therefore, you are no longer strangers and foreigners, but fellow citizens with the saints and members of the household of God, having been built on the foundation of the apostles and prophets, Jesus Christ Himself being the chief cornerstone, in whom the whole building, being fitted together, grows into a holy temple in the Lord, in whom you also are being built together for a dwelling place of God in the Spirit. (Ephesians 2:19-22)

Many people have laid a foundation of belief that is based on a rapture ideology. If the rapture is not really true, they have to re-do the entirety of what they believe. This is a very difficult thing to accomplish. For one thing, it's difficult to admit you are wrong about something. And for another thing, if you've based a good majority of what you believe on something that's false, you have to start over with your beliefs. That seems daunting and scary to people. And yet, that's exactly what needs to be done.

The teaching regarding a rapture is not based on revelation of Jesus, so it is faulty to begin with. And it's a teaching that so overwhelms everything else, that the hope of those who believe in a rapture lies in being raptured out of this world. That's where their hope lies. It's not Jesus in them; it's in Jesus taking them out.

Because the rapture teaching is a lie, it's all based in deception. Therefore, to those who believe it, it looks to them like they're trusting and hoping in Jesus. He's the One they're expecting to save them out of trouble, so they think their hope is in Him. However, their hope is in escape. Jesus didn't escape His tribulations and trials. And He promised we will go through tribulations and trials as well. It was a promise (John 16:33). The testing of our faith through these trials and tribulations brings great reward. Will we overcome by faith, or won't we? Through Jesus we can do all things, and when we trust in Him, we will overcome!

> In this you greatly rejoice, though now for a little while, if need be, you have been grieved by various trials, that the genuineness of your faith, being much more precious than gold that perishes, though it is tested by fire, may be found to praise, honor, and glory at the revelation of Jesus Christ. (1 Peter 1:6-7)

With an understanding of who we are in Christ, who He is in us, and the purpose of the church as a basis, let's look at some of the questions people have regarding Scriptures that have been used to teach a rapture. The first passage comes from 2 Thessalonians 2:1-12.

> Now, brethren, concerning the coming of our Lord Jesus Christ and our gathering together to Him, we ask you, not to be soon shaken in mind or troubled, either by spirit or by word or by letter, as if from us, as though the day of Christ had come. Let no one deceive you by any means; for that Day will not come unless the falling away comes first, and the man of sin is revealed, the son of perdition, who opposes and exalts himself above all that is called God or that is worshiped, so that he sits as God in the temple of God, showing himself that he is God. Do you not remember that when I was still with you I told you these things? And now you know what is restraining, that he may be revealed in his own time. For the mystery of lawlessness is already at work; only he who now restrains will do so until he is taken out of the way. And then the lawless one will be revealed, whom the Lord will consume with the breath of His mouth and destroy with the brightness of His coming. The coming of the lawless one is according to the working of Satan, with all power, signs, and lying wonders, and with all unrighteous deception among those who perish, because they did not receive the love of the truth, that they might be saved. And for this reason God will send them strong delusion, that they should believe the lie, that they all may be condemned who did not believe the truth but had pleasure in unrighteousness.

Some people struggle with understanding the above passage because they have been taught that the church is restraining evil and when the church is taken out of the way, then evil can have its way. However, in these verses Paul is seeing in the spirit. He is seeing lawlessness and a falling away. He is seeing what Jesus prophesied in Matthew 24 about the temple destroyed. He's seeing the near future (20 years out), and he's seeing the very distant future (the Lord's Great Reset and the tares removed). When seeing a vision and hearing prophecy, it can be very easy to put the whole prophecy in one time period, but frequently that is not the case. Instead, the prophecy will happen over time, not all at once. Parts of it may happen at one time and parts at another time.

In this case, the man of lawlessness is not necessarily a man (the Greek word is neutral as far as sex goes). Instead, it's the spirit behind the lawlessness, just as the antichrist is a spirit. John wrote that there are many antichrists in the world.

The Lord says that when the wicked are removed, it's going to get better, better than we've ever dreamed of. That looks like what many refer to as a "millennial reign." It's the Kingdom of Heaven on earth. The evil spirits who have been working in the world Babylon system do not want to be revealed. They don't want us to know what's behind this stuff, that it's demonic. The demonic *wants* to stay hidden.

It's the angels of God who are doing the revealing right now. In particular, the Winds of Change Angel has been blowing the lid off corruption and unmasking deception. As he does this, the spirits of wickedness and the people in agreement with them are revealed and unmasked. The enemy hides behind deception, but when he is revealed, then he can be dealt with and destroyed. That's why Jesus said, **"For everyone practicing evil hates the light and does not come to the light, lest his deeds should be exposed"** (John 3:20).

Therefore, contrary to popular teaching, it's not that the spirits want to be revealed and are waiting for something good to get out of the way so they can be revealed. No! Instead, the demonic does not want to be revealed! They hide behind deception, and it's the light that exposes the darkness so that the power of the darkness can be broken.

Another passage of Scripture used to teach the rapture idea comes from 1 Thessalonians 4:13-18.

> **But I do not want you to be ignorant, brethren, concerning those who have fallen asleep, lest you sorrow as others who have no hope. For if we believe that Jesus died and rose again, even so God will bring with Him those who sleep in Jesus. For this we say to you by the word of the Lord, that we who are alive and remain until the coming of the Lord will by no means precede those who are asleep. For the Lord Himself will descend from heaven with a shout, with the voice of an archangel, and with the trumpet of God. And the dead in Christ will rise first. Then we who are alive and remain shall be caught up together with them in the clouds to meet the Lord in the air. And thus we shall always be with the Lord. Therefore comfort one another with these words.**

Every generation since Jesus ascended to Heaven has believed they were the generation that would welcome the return of the Lord. This is especially true of those who saw Him ascend into Heaven. They were told they would see Him come back in the same way that He had left. They assumed that meant they would be the ones to see Him return. They didn't understand that they might "fall asleep" first, and so it was concerning to them when some of the believers started to die. They were understandably confused because they weren't sure what would happen to those who had died. This concern is what Paul is addressing in 1 Thessalonians 4.

Paul begins Chapter 4 by admonishing the church to keep themselves from sexual immorality because their bodies are holy. He then instructs them to walk in love and peace toward each other and those outside the church. Then Paul addresses the issue of those who have fallen asleep in Christ. (Whenever the phrase "fallen asleep" or something similar to that is used in Scripture it is referring to a believer who has died.) Paul reassures the church that the deceased Christians will be raised up at Christ's return. They will not miss the resurrection of the dead just because they've died. We will all receive our new bodies together, and since those who have preceded us in death are already with the Lord, they will come back with Him to receive their bodies.

Hebrews 11:39-40 (NIV) addresses the believers who have gone before us. It says, **"These were all commended for their faith, yet none of them received what had been promised. God had planned something better for us so that only together with us would they be made perfect."** In other words, they didn't receive the resurrection of their bodies yet, but will do so with us who are left on the earth when Jesus returns.

Going back to 1 Thessalonians, let's continue into Chapter 5. Remember when you are reading these letters, they are letters and were not written in chapters. So, what Paul is writing about doesn't end at the end of Chapter 4 but continues into Chapter 5.

> **But concerning the times and the seasons, brethren, you have no need that I should write to you. For you yourselves know perfectly that the day of the Lord so comes as a thief in the night. For when they say, "Peace and safety!" then sudden destruction comes upon them, as labor pains upon a pregnant woman. And they shall not escape. But you, brethren, are not in darkness, so that this Day should overtake you as a thief. You are all sons of light and sons of**

the day. We are not of the night nor of darkness. Therefore let us not sleep, as others do, but let us watch and be sober. For those who sleep, sleep at night, and those who get drunk are drunk at night. But let us who are of the day be sober, putting on the breastplate of faith and love, and as a helmet the hope of salvation. For God did not appoint us to wrath, but to obtain salvation through our Lord Jesus Christ, who died for us, that whether we wake or sleep, we should live together with Him. Therefore comfort each other and edify one another, just as you also are doing. (1 Thessalonians 5:1-11)

The proponents of a rapture point to verse 9 where Paul writes that God did not appoint us to wrath. That is correct. If you are in Christ, the wrath of God is *not* on you! However, Paul is not teaching about being raptured so that you escape wrath. You escape wrath by being in Christ, not by escaping out of the world.

Instead of teaching about a rapture, Paul is teaching the way of holiness so that we do not walk in darkness. We are the sons of light and are supposed to walk as though we are in the light. We do not participate in the evil deeds of darkness like those who come under the wrath of God. Jesus became sin for us so that we might become the righteousness of God in Him (2 Corinthians 5:21). Because of this, we are appointed not to wrath, but to salvation through Jesus Christ in order that whether we are alive or "asleep," we may live with Christ. Therefore, to be "caught up" together with those who have gone before us simply means that the body of Christ will be joined together when He comes again.

Whatever is not of Jesus will be shaken and destroyed. Faith suffers when it's not in Christ because our faith is to be only on the Rock, who is Jesus. Only He can stand and make us stand. We just need to listen to the LORD. All the time, the Holy Spirit leads us into all truth. Therefore, we preach Jesus and Him crucified, not raptured.

When Jesus returns, it will be obvious. Matthew 24:27 says, **"For as lightning that comes from the east is visible even in the west, so will be the coming of the Son of Man."** In other words, His return will be visible. You will be able to see it. There won't be a sneaky return that you may miss or a sneaky return to grab some people and then leave and come back later for a third return. There is only one more return, and Jesus specifically warned His followers not to believe He was coming back until after the tribulation of the last days. He says in Matthew 24:26, 29-30,

> **"Therefore, if they say to you, 'Look, He is in the desert!' do not go out; or 'Look, He is in the inner rooms!' do not believe it... Immediately after the tribulation of those days the sun will be darkened, and the moon will not give its light; the stars will fall from heaven, and the powers of the heavens will be shaken. Then the sign of the Son of Man will appear in heaven, and then all the tribes of the earth will mourn, and they will see the Son of Man coming on the clouds of heaven with power and great glory."**

So Jesus warns us not to be fooled by those who say He's coming before a tribulation of any sort. He's not. This is evident in Hebrews 9:28, which reads, **"... so Christ was offered once to bear the sins of many. To those who eagerly wait for Him He will appear a second time, apart from sin, for salvation."** He's not coming a sneaky second time and then a third time. The Bible clearly says He's coming only a second time, since He's already been here the first time.

The fact that Jesus will return not for sin, but for salvation is also why Paul discourses to the Thessalonians in 1 Thessalonians 4:13-5:11 that they shouldn't sorrow or lose hope when a brother or sister dies. For we'll see them again because Jesus will come in an obvious manner, judge the wicked, and gather the faithful to Him for our salvation. That's why he says in 1 Thessalonians 5:9 that we are not appointed to wrath, but to salvation. Jesus' second coming means a person will either experience wrath or salvation. When we're in Christ, our destiny is salvation.

The Prophet Malachi prophesied that the Lord would send Elijah before the coming of the LORD. The three apostles on the Mount of Transfiguration were confused about this because they saw Elijah with Jesus on the mountain, yet the prophecy said Elijah would come before the Messiah. Jesus answered them by explaining that Elijah did come, meaning John the Baptist, and that Elijah would come, meaning the church. John came in the Spirit of Elijah because Elijah came by the power of the Spirit of Prophecy – who is the Holy Spirit. Jesus could say that Elijah would still come because the Holy Spirit had not yet been poured out at that point. But when He was, those who received Him would prepare the way for the Lord's second coming.

Additionally, Jesus is coming back for a bride who He has made holy, who is mature and complete, and who is united in faith and in the knowledge of the Son of God. This bride is not weak, immature, and unable to handle tribulation. This bride is like her Husband, is one with Him, and is strong, filled with faith, mature, able, and a victor. Jesus said that the gates of hell would not prevail against His church (Matthew 16:18). How then could we possibly believe that things would get so bad He would have to take us out of the earth?

Besides that, Jesus is the Head of His church. If the church can't handle something, then Jesus loses. Is that even possible? Of course not! Jesus never loses! He's already won!

As of 2023, we are in a great tribulation. The Lord will deliver us out of it. He has promised we would go through tribulations, but that our hope is in Him. In all of this we are more than conquerors through Him who loves us, and our faith will be proved pure and strong as we continue to stand in faith and believe the LORD!

We are supposed to be on the offense, taking ground for the Kingdom of Heaven, and preparing the way for the return of the LORD. We are the head and not the tail. We are victorious and not defeated. We are the ones with authority and power. The enemy is nothing, and Jesus is everything! In Him we will never be defeated! The earth is the LORD's and all its fullness! (Psalm 24:1) We're not giving it to the enemy and we're not believing that anything will ever be so bad that through the power of the Holy Spirit, we just can't take it anymore and have to be taken out of the earth. No way! We are more than conquerors through Him who loved us! (Romans 8:37) Jesus has made us kings and priests to our God, and we shall reign on the earth! (Revelation 5:10) Halleluiah!

Let's turn to the Parable of the Wheat and the Tares in which Jesus said that the wheat and tares would grow together until the time of the harvest (Matthew 13:24-30, 36-43). At the time of maturity, the tares would be removed and burned first. Then the wheat would be harvested. The tares are the sons of the wicked one. They are the ones who do wickedly on the earth. The wheat are the sons of God, those who are in Christ. The parable that Jesus told and explained clearly goes against the idea of a rapture. There is no removing of the wheat – the sons of God – before a tribulation. Instead, the evil ones – the tares – are removed.

Now, let's look at the Parable of the Mustard Seed.

Another parable He put forth to them, saying: "The kingdom of heaven is like a mustard seed, which a man took and sowed in his field, which indeed is the least of all the seeds; but when it is grown

it is greater than the herbs and becomes a tree, so that the birds of the air come and nest in its branches. (Matthew 13:31-32)

In this parable, the Kingdom of Heaven takes over. It doesn't escape or shrink back or become defeated. In fact, there's nothing that can overcome it. The same is true in the Parable of the Leaven.

Another parable He spoke to them: "The kingdom of heaven is like leaven, which a woman took and hid in three measures of meal till it was all leavened." (Matthew 13:33)

Again, the Kingdom of Heaven takes over. And where is the Kingdom of God? It is within you! (Luke 17:21) Those who carry the Holy Spirit, bring the Kingdom of Heaven everywhere they go. The leaven of God works through all the seven mountains in the earth (Family, Government, Economy & Business, Arts & Entertainment, Religion, Education, and Media), and in every nation! Those who carry the Kingdom bring light. They bring life. They bring Jesus and His rule and reign everywhere they go by the power of His Spirit in them.

The whole idea of a rapture goes against the very nature of God. Rapturing people out of trouble is not how God does things. He doesn't rapture us out of tribulation and suffering and persecution. Instead, He gives us grace, which is empowerment.

All we need to do is look at Jesus. Even Jesus didn't get raptured out. He asked to escape the wrath coming and God told Him no. If Father was going to let anyone be raptured, it would have been Jesus. But He didn't. And if we are willing to suffer with Christ, we will also be glorified with Him.

The Spirit Himself bears witness with our spirit that we are children of God, and if children, then heirs – heirs of God and

35

> **joint heirs with Christ, if indeed we suffer with Him, that we may also be glorified together.** (Romans 8:16-17)

We will suffer with Christ if we are heirs of God. It's an honor to participate in the suffering of Christ. It brings with it a weight of glory. When we are broken, Christ shines through. Where we have died, Jesus lives. We rejoice that Jesus counts us worthy to suffer for His name. Do not fear!

Who are your eyes on if you're thinking about a rapture? Self. *I'm going to escape.* Your eyes are not on Jesus and desiring an unblemished bride for Him if you're thinking of escaping hardship. Your eyes are not on bringing His kingdom to earth if you're trying to check out. The end times church will be dead to self, not concerned with being raptured out of anything. Rapture is attractive to those who are concerned about self, suffering, and persecution. When we've died to self, a rapture is not attractive anymore.

The whole creation waits for the sons of God to be revealed because we're supposed to be bringing Heaven to earth (Romans 8). Escaping is all about preserving self, and Jesus said that those who love their lives would lose them. But those who lose their lives for Him would save them.

While the early church and all the believers since Christ's ascension have looked for His return and thought that it would be in their days, they were not looking to be raptured out of trouble. Jesus said that we would undergo tribulation, but to take heart because He has overcome the world (John 16:33). Because He overcame, we too can overcome through His Spirit that lives in us. We must see ourselves in Christ and Him in us. We must see that we are more than conquerors through Him who loves us. We must keep our eyes on Jesus and not look to be bailed out of trouble.

People may get angry with you if you question their beliefs regarding a rapture because their belief is not based on revelation, but on opinion and the doctrine of demons. When you have an opinion, you have to defend it. This is why opinions are a trap. It leads to needless arguing and strife. The same is true when you believe in a lie through the deception of the enemy. You can't really defend the lie through the power of the Holy Spirit. You have to intellectualize and figure out how the lie is right. It's stressful and causes frustration and anger, which is basically based in insecurity because of the faulty foundation. When you base what you believe on revelation, however, the Holy Spirit will give you what to say and what to do in the moment. You don't have to depend on yourself. The knowledge of the truth is within you.

Unless someone is willing to throw out the whole rapture teaching and start new, they will continue to be deceived and may become angry when you speak with them on the subject. You, however, will base your beliefs on the revelation of Jesus revealed to you through His Spirit as spoken by His apostles and prophets. Your foundation will be sure, and you will not feel the need to become angry or frustrated if people question you. Rather than looking to be raptured out of trouble, let's look to take over the darkness through the Holy Spirit of Christ who lives in us!

Jesus' focus for His disciples was that they would be filled with the Holy Spirit, make disciples of the nations, and bring the Kingdom of Heaven to earth. We're here to make a difference in the earth. We're not here to live for self, or live in fear, or look for escape. We're here to bring the nations to the Lord. Let's fix our eyes on Jesus and go forward! (See Romans 8:37, Matthew 28:18-20, Hebrews 12:1-2.)

Quit thinking about leaving and start thinking about taking over.

CHAPTER 4

TRIBULATION & PERSECUTION

W e mentioned briefly in the last chapter that we escape the wrath of God by being in Christ. However, some people believe that we will escape all tribulation and persecution by being in Christ or by being raptured. However, Jesus didn't teach escape from tribulation or persecution. He prayed in John 17:15, "**I do not pray that You should take them out of the world, but that You should keep them from the evil one.**" In other words, Jesus wasn't praying for us to escape out of the world, but that we would be kept from the devil's ways and traps.

Some who believe we will escape tribulation and persecution use Luke 21:36 as "proof" that a rapture will take place. It reads, "**Watch therefore, and pray always that you may be counted worthy to escape all these things that will come to pass, and to stand before the Son of Man.**" However, Jesus wasn't saying to pray that we'd be able to escape the tribulation. Read the verses before this and you will see what you are to pray you will escape from:

> "**Be careful, or your hearts will be weighed down with dissipation, drunkenness and the anxieties of life, and that day will close on you unexpectedly like a trap. For it will come upon all those who live on the face of the earth.**" (v. 34-35, NIV)

In other words, Jesus wants us to escape the sins of dissipation, drunkenness and the anxieties of life. This goes back to His prayer in John 17 that we would be kept from the evil one.

In Revelation 18:4 God tells His people to come out of Babylon so we don't receive her plagues or share in her sins. We are to come out of the world's system and into the Lord's Kingdom. Additionally, these things will come upon all who live on the earth, but we don't have to be weighed down by it. We need to keep our eyes on Jesus and remain standing. Those who stand will remain.

Instead of being taken out of the world, we are encouraged in 1 Timothy 6:13-15 to keep the faith until Christ's return:

> I urge you in the sight of God who gives life to all things, and before Christ Jesus who witnessed the good confession before Pontius Pilate, that you keep this commandment without spot, blameless until our Lord Jesus Christ's appearing, which He will manifest in His own time, He who is the blessed and only Potentate, the King of kings and Lord of lords . . .

During times of tribulation those who stay close to the Lord will not be moved by the tribulation. This is what Isaiah is referring to in the following passage:

> Your dead shall live;
> Together with my dead body they shall arise.
> Awake and sing, you who dwell in dust;
> For your dew is like the dew of herbs,
> And the earth shall cast out the dead.
> Come, my people, enter your chambers,
> And shut your doors behind you;
> Hide yourself, as it were, for a little moment,
> Until the indignation is past.
> For behold, the LORD comes out of His place
> To punish the inhabitants of the earth for their iniquity;
> The earth will also disclose her blood;
> And will no more cover her slain. (Isaiah 26:19-21)

When we are hidden in Christ, there is no more wrath for us. Jesus bore the wrath of God for us. Father says that His anger toward us would be like the waters of Noah to Him. Just as He would not allow the waters to cover the earth again, so He will not be angry with us or rebuke us (Isaiah 54:9). When we are born again, we are hidden in Christ. God is no longer angry with us. His wrath is not on us.

However, we are told we will suffer for the name of Christ. We are told we will endure persecution and we're to consider it all joy because the testing of our faith develops perseverance and perseverance character and character hope and hope does not disappoint us (Romans 5:4). We will endure many afflictions as we stand for Jesus, so we need to persevere and encourage each other.

> . . . so that we ourselves boast of you among the churches of God for your patience and faith in all your persecutions and tribulations that you endure, which is manifest evidence of the righteous judgment of God, that you may be counted worthy of the kingdom of God, for which you also suffer; since it is a righteous thing with God to repay with tribulation those who trouble you, and to give you who are troubled rest with us when the Lord Jesus is revealed from heaven with His mighty angels, in flaming fire taking vengeance on those who do not know God, and on those who do not obey the gospel of our Lord Jesus Christ. These shall be punished with everlasting destruction from the presence of the Lord and from the glory of His power, when he comes, in that Day, to be glorified among all those who believe, because our testimony among you was believed. This includes you, because you believed our testimony to you. (2 Thessalonians 1:4-10)

Notice that Paul makes it clear that when we suffer for Jesus we are being counted worthy of the Kingdom of God. We are not under His wrath, but we are promised persecution and suffering. To endure that with faith and love is to win and receive a reward. It's an honor to suffer for the name of Jesus. We are the light of the world because the Light lives in us. Darkness cannot overcome us, no matter how much it tries to persecute us.

Jesus says in Revelation 3:10, **"Because you have kept My command to persevere, I also will keep you from the hour of trial which shall come upon the whole world, to test those who dwell on the earth."** This verse is footnoted with John 16:15, which is part of Jesus' prayer for us, namely His disciples, and it reads: **"I do not pray that You should take them out of the world, but that You should keep them from the evil one."** God will not take us out of the world to escape the tribulation. He knows how to take care of His own and we can rest in Him. We need only follow Him and not fear. His wrath is not on the righteous.

So, has the "Great Tribulation" happened already or not? Jesus said in Matthew 24:21, **"For then there will be great tribulation, such as has not been since the beginning of the world until this time, no nor ever shall be."**

Jesus prophesied of "great tribulation" at a time when the temple would be torn down. There have been many "great tribulations" on the earth since He prophesied this. But the great tribulation that Jesus prophesied in Matthew 24 happened between 64 AD and 70 AD. The Christians alive at that time knew that what they were experiencing was what Jesus had prophesied. Because they believed Him, their lives were spared.

A little before 66 AD, the antisemitism of the ruling Romans became so oppressive that the Jews in Jerusalem stormed the Antonia Fortress and killed the Romans stationed there. This started a war with Rome which ended with Jerusalem in ruins, the temple completely torn down with only a portion of the outer wall of the temple mount still standing, which is now called the "wailing wall," over a million Jews dead, and the nation of Israel no longer a nation.

Here are some of the highlights that happened in 66 AD, to give you an idea of just how great a tribulation this time was.

- The Roman Governor of Judea, Gessius Florus, murdered around 3,600 Jews with about 2,000 of them being crucified.
- The Romans of Caesarea killed around 20,000 Jews.
- Around 10,000 Jews were murdered in Damascus, Syria.
- It is reported that there was infighting among the Jews of at least three different factions, where each leader claimed to be the messiah.
- There were numerous earthquakes.

Then in 70 AD Emperor Vespasian's son Titus came and broke down the walls around Jerusalem, slaughtered the inhabitants, and completely destroyed the temple, leaving no stone on another.

The astonishing thing about this bit of history is that it is reported by historians, like Jospehus, that no Christian died in what is referred to as the "Battle of the Jews." Instead of dying in the fighting, the Christians took the prophecy of Jesus literally. As they saw the signs that Jesus prophesied coming to pass, they fled Jerusalem in 66 AD to Pella and other places where they were safe from the slaughter and final destruction of Jerusalem in 70 AD.

The facts of this time in history can be easily found through internet searches and historical books, especially those written by Josephus, who lived through the Roman conquest of Jerusalem.

It should be obvious when reading Jesus' prophesy of "great tribulation" and then reading the history of what happened to the nation of Israel only 37 years afterwards, that what Jesus prophesied has come to pass.

The Christians who were living at the time fled Jerusalem because of what Jesus prophesied, and because of this, they lived. They knew they were living in great tribulation, and they obeyed the words of the Lord.

Because some people think there should be a different outcome to the prophecy, they say it hasn't happened yet, but it surely has. Those who lived through it knew it, and when we look back at history, we know it has happened as well. There was great tribulation from 64-70 AD, just as Jesus said there would be. A quick timeline can be found at: Time Line AD 30 - 70 (agapebiblestudy.com). [We do not promote or approve of everything on this website.]

Even though a great tribulation happened shortly after Jesus prophesied it would, there have been other tribulations as well. Jesus even prophesied we are in a great tribulation right now. In fact, He has gone so far as to say that evil will never rise to this level again on the earth. The enemy has been working on a world system of evil for centuries, and probably longer than that. Yet, God's plan is to completely destroy the works of the devil and bring about the Great Reset of the LORD.

Here are a few of the prophetic words the Holy Spirit has given to us regarding this tribulation and the goodness of God in totally destroying the evil world system.

The Lord asked which of these things [in Matthew 24 & 25 and 1 Timothy 3] is not happening right now? I said that I thought all of the things that I read about were happening right now. He said: "That's correct. Could you really say to the Coptic Christians, the Chinese Christians, or the Christians living in Pakistan or many other places on the earth that things were going to get much, much worse? Worse than mass beheadings, burning alive, drowning, etc.? Could you say child sacrifice is going to get much, much worse? (There were 40,892,880 abortions this year in the world so far on December 16,

2021, at 6:40 p.m.) Could you say that those who control the world economy, the nations of the world, really the world itself will get much, much worse? Even though they are under Satan himself, and as such endorse any and all kinds of sin, some we have never heard of yet! There are other things we could talk about, things that are so foolish regarding sex, sports, health, the welfare system, and arts & entertainment. Is there anything, including the so-called church that isn't broken and corrupt?"

*The Lord has said that He is on a rescue mission and that **things would never get this bad again**. Corruption will be exposed. Evil will be punished because justice is His foundation of His throne! Amen.* (*How Much Worse Will it Get Prophecy,* December 16, 2021)

*"We're almost there. Time is short. Open your heart in love, and yet the law must be followed and applied to those who are found guilty by it. Look around you. Remember what it was like to be enslaved by the evil one! Look one more time! **Because things will never be like this again!** Ever!*

I AM says today that these changes are <u>not</u> for one place or one people! I AM on a rescue mission, and it is for the whole world! The United States, yes! But the ripples from what I accomplish there will flow around the entire planet. Amen!" (*Dangerous & Confusing Time Prophecy,* July 26, 2022)

"When I send a Prophet to the people to warn them of what is to come, to tell them to avoid the coming evil which might befall them, they believe it and regard the Prophet highly! Conversely, when I send a Prophet a message of the good which I have planned for My people, they call him a fake prophet! They believe the world can only become worse than it is currently. They speak to one another about the future in a lament! Yes, Even My obedient ones have taken an attitude of being defeated! They say within themselves that it will never get better! Each

one who does this is prophesying their own doom. I, the Lord, say, 'Look up for your redemption draws near!' and they look down at the ground...

This should not be My people! Am I too weak to change things? Is My goodness not good enough? Is not My justice just? Answer Me you who can only 'see' a bleak future! I Am requiring an answer! I Am requiring a change of attitude and belief! I, even I, have never failed! I will not be seen as a failure either!

Fear has to be 'put out' of your lives, out of your belief system. I Am the Lord. Faith must be 'put on' every morning and carried during the day. I will NEVER leave you or forsake you! I will hold you up by My strong right hand! Rise up in your most holy faith! I long to pour out My grace (empowerment) to help you! I love each one of you. Amen." (*God is Good Prophecy,* July 20, 2021)

Each of these prophetic words addresses either how evil will never rise to this level again and/or how for some reason people have a difficult time believing that things are going to get better and not worse.

The definition of tribulation is:

1. Great affliction, trial or distress;
2. An experience that tests one's endurance, patience, or faith;
3. A state of affliction or oppression; suffering; distress.
(The American Heritage® Dictionary of the English Language, 5th Edition.)

A servant is not above his master. If Jesus went through tribulation, we will too. He promises we will. Jesus was harassed, they picked up stones to stone Him at one point, He was thought to be out of His mind by His own family, some of His disciples left Him because His teachings were too hard, He was betrayed by one of the twelve, He was spit upon, mocked, beaten, whipped, and finally crucified. Sounds like tribulation. Jesus said,

> "Behold, I send you out as sheep in the midst of wolves. Therefore be wise as serpents and harmless as doves. But beware of men, for they will deliver you up to councils and scourge you in their synagogues. You will be brought before governors and kings for My sake, as a testimony to them and to the Gentiles. But when they deliver you up, do not worry about how or what you should speak. For it will be given to you in that hour what you should speak; for it is not you who speak, but the Spirit of your Father who speaks in you. Now brother will deliver up brother to death, and a father his child; and children will rise up against parents and cause them to be put to death. And you will be hated by all for My name's sake. But he who endures to the end will be saved. When they persecute you in this city, flee to another. For assuredly, I say to you, you will not have gone through the cities of Israel before the Son of Man comes. A disciple is not above his teacher, nor a servant above his master. It is enough for a disciple that he be like his teacher, and a servant like his master. If they have called the master of the house Beelzebub, how much more will they call those of his household! Therefore do not fear them. For there is nothing covered that will not be revealed, and hidden that will not be known." (Matthew 10:16-26)

All of the things Jesus mentioned in the above Scripture happened to the first church and continues to happen today. Peter and John were put in jail for healing a lame man in Acts 3 and 4, the apostles were imprisoned in Acts 5, Stephen was stoned to death in Acts 8, Saul was creating havoc and imprisoning believers in Acts 8, the Apostle James the brother of John was killed by Herod in Acts 12, Peter was imprisoned in Acts 12, and the list goes on and on.

Today's believers are treated no better in many parts of the world. They are harassed, persecuted, have their homes destroyed and belongings taken away, they are denied good employment, they are mocked, hunted down, beaten, imprisoned, tortured, beheaded, and killed in various ways. How many of you have family members that turned against you when you truly decided to follow the Holy Spirit? How many of you got kicked out of churches for not conforming to their mold? How many of you suffer in other ways because you decided to believe various promises from the Lord?

If you don't believe tribulation occurs where you live, look to other areas of the world where it does occur regularly. *The Heavenly Man* by Brother Yun is a great example of a modern-day believer being persecuted. Or you need only pick up a *Voice of the Martyrs* magazine to read the accounts of believers today suffering for the name of Jesus.

Each generation of believers is persecuted for the name of Jesus and must decide to keep believing or give up. Tribulation serves to purify our faith, just as fire purifies gold. And our faith is worth much more than gold. Jesus did not escape tribulation, and if we follow Him, we will not either. He says to us, **"In this world you will have trouble. But take heart! I have overcome the world."** (John 16:33, NIV)

The Apostle John also testified of persecution. **"I, John, both your brother and companion in the tribulation and kingdom and patience of Jesus Christ, was on the island that is called Patmos for the word of God and for the testimony of Jesus Christ."** (Revelation 1:9)

There's tribulation because of the Kingdom of the LORD. The Kingdom of Heaven suffers violence and the violent take it by force. The enemy does not want the Kingdom of Heaven established on earth. Hence, he causes trouble and resists it. Yet, love never fails and with faith all things are possible. So we have tribulation, the kingdom, and patience all at once as we establish the will of God on earth, just as John testifies.

In all of this, we are more than conquerors through Him who loves us! (Romans 8:37) So, take heart, and look at these things with eyes of victory, not defeat.

CHAPTER 5

JESUS' END TIMES TEACHINGS

———————— ◆ ◂◂ ◈ ▸▸ ◆ ————————

Jesus had several teachings and prophecies about the end times. For example, Jesus prophesied the destruction of the temple at a time when Jerusalem would be surrounded by armies.

> Then, as some spoke of the temple, how it was adorned with beautiful stones and donations, He said, "These things which you see – the days will come in which not one stone shall be left upon another that shall not be thrown down… But when you see Jerusalem surrounded by armies, then know that its destruction is near. Then let those who are in Judea flee to the mountains, let those who are in the midst of her depart, and let not those who are in the country enter her. For these are the days of vengeance, that all things which are written may be fulfilled. But woe to those who are pregnant and to those who are nursing babies in those days! For there will be great distress on the land and wrath upon this people. And they will fall by the edge of the sword, and be led away captive into all nations. And Jerusalem will be trampled by Gentiles until the times of the Gentiles are fulfilled." (Luke 21:5-6, 20-24)

It's important to note that this is not a future event, but it's something that actually happened in 70 AD. The temple was torn down without a stone left on another, Jerusalem was destroyed, and the Jews were slaughtered to such an extent that Josephus reported you couldn't see the ground because of the blood from those who were killed.

Because some of the other things Jesus prophesied have not happened yet, like His return, many people teach that the temple has to be built again and then Jerusalem surrounded again and then the temple and Jerusalem destroyed again. This is a fallacy. Jesus prophesied in Luke 21:9 that the **"end will not come immediately"** after the things that come to pass first. And He said in verse 28, **"Now when these things begin to happen, look up and lift up your heads, because your redemption draws near."** He said when these things "begin" to happen.

Have you ever noticed that prophecy doesn't generally happen immediately, nor all at once? Instead of giving us exact dates for each event, the Lord tends to give us signs of seasons so that we are forced to use our faith. For example, He says in Luke 21:29-31, **"Look at the fig tree, and all the trees. When they are already budding, you see and know for yourselves that summer is now near. So you also, when you see these things happening, know that the kingdom of God is near."**

Therefore, just because some of the prophecy has not come to pass, does not mean that the parts that have come to pass have to happen again at the same time as the rest of the prophecy. That doesn't even make sense. A long prophecy given at one time does not mean that the entire prophecy has to come to pass all at once. The temple was destroyed without a stone left on another in 70 AD. This part of Jesus' prophecy has been fulfilled. We do not have to wait for another temple to be built and torn down again. It has already happened.

Besides that, even if a new temple was built and it housed the ark of the covenant and other items from the past, it would not be "holy." God does not reside in buildings, but in men through His Spirit. The Kingdom of Heaven is within you. Praise Jesus!

There are still many events that have occurred that Jesus prophesied would happen. We'll go through several, but first let's look at Luke

21:19. Jesus said, **"By your patience possess your souls."** Jesus was telling us to have control over our souls through patience. This is because we need to be patient! Prophecy does not always happen all at once, or in the timing we think it should. Through this the Lord teaches us to have faith and patience. For example, Jesus told John in Revelation that He was coming "soon." That was two thousand years ago. Soon to God is not necessarily soon to us. Is God going to change, or should we change to agree with Him? Therefore, with patience, we can continue to look at the things that have happened and the things that are yet to come.

In Matthew 24:6-7, Jesus says, **"And you will hear of wars and rumors of wars. See that you are not troubled; for all of these things must come to pass, but the end is not yet. For nation will rise against nation, and kingdom against kingdom. And there will be famines, pestilences, and earthquakes in various places."** As Jesus prophesied, there have been wars and rumors of wars, earthquakes, and famines at various times in history since Jesus prophesied this. However, this was not supposed to concern the disciples. Instead, they were to look for the point when Jerusalem was surrounded by armies to flee the country without taking time to pack. This actually happened when Cestius Gallus surrounded Jerusalem.

Gallus was a general in the Roman army, and evidently governor of Syria. He was called on to quell the Jewish revolt. While he did some damage to the Jews and their lands, he mysteriously pulled his troops back from breaking through the wall to Jerusalem and retreated. During his retreat, he was attacked by the Jewish forces to such an extent that he lost an alleged 5,300 men (NERO'S WAR I: THE BLUNDER OF CESTIUS GALLUS? (Chapter 5) - A History of the Jewish War (cambridge.org) Even if this was not the exact number of men, he was considered defeated.

The Christians took the opportunity afforded them by Gallus' retreat to flee to Pella. By the time Titus came in 70 AD and destroyed Jerusalem and the temple, the Christians were gone. They had believed the prophecy of Jesus and fled. Had they dawdled in order to pack or set things right before they left, they wouldn't have had time to escape.

Jesus further went on to prophesy that Jerusalem would be destroyed, and the disciples should specifically flee to the mountains. If they fled to the city for refuge, like they would normally do when armies came, they would perish. The believers in Christ obeyed what Jesus had commanded and fled to Pella, which is in the foothills of the Transjordanian Mountains, and they miraculously survived the slaughter of the Jews when Jerusalem was destroyed in 70 AD. Therefore, these prophecies were fulfilled.

Within this prophecy, Jesus said, **"And pray that your flight may not be in winter or on the Sabbath."** This prophecy only makes sense in a time when the Law was in full effect, which was at the time of the destruction of the holy city and the temple. Their escape would be hampered by those who may prevent them from "breaking the Sabbath" if their flight happened on the Sabbath. Hence, they prayed, and were able to escape when the siege lifted without it being winter or the Sabbath. Another prophecy fulfilled.

Jesus also prophesied that His disciples would be delivered to the councils, put in prison, beat in the synagogues, and that their persecution would turn out as an opportunity for testimony. (Mark 13:9, Luke 21:13) You need only to flip over to the book of Acts and start reading in Chapter 4 through the rest of the Bible to see this happening. The apostles and other disciples of Christ were repeatedly brought before the councils, put in jail, flogged, and beaten, left for dead, and eventually killed. Neither Peter nor Paul lived to see the destruction of Jerusalem because they were both martyred before it happened. And yet, as Jesus prophesied, they used the opportunity of persecution to give testimony of Jesus Christ. (See Acts 26 for an example of this when Paul spoke to King Agrippa.) And they weren't the only ones. James, Stephen, and many others were martyred before this event took place.

Much of what Jesus prophesied would happen has happened. Jesus said, **"Now when these things begin to happen, look up and lift up your heads, because your redemption draws near."** (Luke 21:28) These things have begun to happen just as Jesus prophesied they would.

When we consider the end times, we must always look at what Jesus has said. In the parable of the wheat and the tares, Jesus clearly lays out how things will work during the end times.

> Another parable He put forth to them, saying: "The Kingdom of heaven is like a man who sowed good seed in his field; but while men slept, his enemy came and sowed tares among the wheat and went his way. But when the grain had sprouted and produced a crop, then the tares also appeared. So the servants of the owner came and said to him, 'Sir, did you not sow good seed in your field? How then does it have tares?' He said to them, 'An enemy has done this.' The servants said to him, 'Do you want us then to go and gather them up?' But he said, 'No, lest while you gather up the tares you also uproot the wheat with them. Let both grow together until the harvest, and at the time of harvest I will say to the reapers, 'First gather together the tares and bind them in bundles to burn them, but gather the wheat into my barn.'" (Matthew 24-30)

Then Jesus sent the multitude away and went into the house. And His disciples came to Him, saying, "Explain to us the parable of the tares of the field." He answered and said to them: "He who sows the good seed is the Son of Man. The field is the world, the good seeds are the sons of the kingdom, but the tares are the sons of the wicked one. The enemy who sowed them is the devil, the harvest is the end of the age, and the reapers are the angels. Therefore as the tares are gathered and burned in the fire, so it will be at the end of this age. The Son of Man will send out His angels, and they will gather out of His kingdom all things that offend, and those who practice lawlessness, and will cast them into the furnace of fire. There will be wailing and gnashing of teeth. Then the righteous will shine forth as the sun in the kingdom of their Father. He who has ears to hear, let him hear!" (Matthew 13:36-43)

This is what the end of the age will look like because God has spoken this parable, and also its interpretation. It is according to Jesus how it will be at the end of the age. This parable and its interpretation form a baseline for what the end of the age will look like.

Take note that Jesus says specifically that the wheat should not be gathered before the tares, and specifically does say that the tares should be gathered by the angels at the end of the age, then the wheat. Other Scriptures regarding "the end of the age" or Jesus' second coming will agree with this. If it is interpreted differently, or a doctrine is formed in opposition to what Jesus clearly taught, it is wrong.

The disciples had asked Jesus when the Kingdom of God would come and what would be the sign of His coming again. He responded by saying that they wouldn't miss it when He came back, but that they should look for certain events to happen to know that the time was near. One of the things they were to watch for was that things would be similar to the time of Noah's day before the flood.

"And as it was in the days of Noah, so it will be also in the days of the Son of Man: They ate, they drank, they married wives, they were given in marriage, until the day that Noah entered the ark, and the flood came and destroyed them all." (Luke 17:26-27)

Jesus said the wicked ones didn't know **"until the flood came and took them all away, so also will the coming of the Son of Man be."** (Matthew 24:39) He then went on to describe that people would be working together and sleeping together and doing other things together, and suddenly the wicked would be taken out, just as the flood came and took out the wicked in Noah's day (Matthew 24:40-44).

In the time of Noah before the flood came and destroyed all the evil people in the world, the people were living life like they always had. The world was going on just as it seemed to have always done. Those of the world were doing all the things they would normally do. They had no concern that something was going to happen to them. Instead, they were eating, drinking, partying, getting married, basically doing everything that would indicate that they believed life would continue on for them as it had been for a long time. This was all despite the fact that Noah was building an ark in front of their eyes and had been for 100 years, and that while he built the ark, he was preaching righteousness (2 Peter 2:5).

The righteous, however, were preparing for a change. The righteous were ready for something big to happen. The righteous had the Lord's perspective and were in obedience to the Lord. Therefore, when the flood came, the wicked were taken out, and the righteous remained.

Keeping this account of what happened in Noah's day in mind, we then have to consider what the Lord's agenda is. What is His plan? He told us the Wheat and Tares parable is the foundation of our end times theology. How does the time of Noah fit into that? Jesus tells us right here who is removed when He returns. It is not the righteous. It is the wicked – all those who offend. This is just what He did with Sodom and Gomorrah. Who was removed from earth? Not Lot. It was all the wicked in Sodom and Gomorrah. Who was removed from the earth in the days of Noah? Not Noah. Noah was righteous. He remained, but the wicked in the earth were completely destroyed and removed. It's just like when the angels come and take the tares and burn them. They are taking the unrighteous away and leaving the righteous to rule and reign with Christ.

God is not giving the earth over to the evil one. Jesus is coming back to take it! It's strange to think that we would give our lives to bring Heaven to Earth and then leave and hand it all over to the devil. We will see the wicked taken out, and the righteous remain to flood the earth with the knowledge of the glory of the Lord as the waters cover the seas (Habakkuk 2:14). This is exactly what the Lord has prophesied repeatedly regarding His Great Reset.

The disciples then asked where this would happen, and Jesus said wherever there's a body, there the eagles are. (Luke 17:37) The eagles represent the apostles, so wherever the church is, the tares will be found and will be removed, just as the wicked were removed in Noah's day.

This will come as a surprise to the wicked, but it shouldn't be a surprise to the righteous. We can look around us and see these things beginning to happen already. By the Spirit of the Lord Jesus Christ, we can discern the times we're in and see that is very similar to the days of Noah. We're surrounded by wickedness that the Lord says He is removing, and the Lord has prophesied a Great Reset where things will never get this bad again. He's also said that He's doing a new thing. He desires His people to join Him in the front lines of the battle, to take over the seven mountains of influence that He will likely end up bringing down to three, and so much more!

Jesus also spoke of separating the sheep and goats. When will this happen, and what does this have to do with His perfect bride? Let's look at Matthew 25:31-46.

> "When the Son of Man comes in His glory, and all the holy angels with Him, then He will sit on the throne of His glory. All the nations will be gathered before Him, and He will separate them one from another, as a shepherd divides his sheep from the goats. And he will set the sheep on His right hand, but the goats on the left. Then the King will say to those on His right hand, 'Come, you blessed of My Father, inherit the kingdom prepared for you from the foundation of the world: for I was hungry and you gave Me food; I was thirsty and you gave Me drink; I was a stranger and you took Me in; I was naked and you clothed Me; I was sick and you visited Me; I was in prison and you came to Me.' Then the righteous will answer Him saying, 'Lord, when did we see You hungry and feed You, or thirsty and give You drink? When did we see You a stranger and take You in, or naked and clothe You? Or when did we see You sick, or in prison, and come to You?' And the King will answer and say to them, 'Assuredly, I say to you, inasmuch as you did it to one of the least of these My brethren, you did it to Me.'" (Matthew 25:31-40)

Jesus goes on to tell them that those who did not do these things for Him will go into everlasting punishment (Matthew 25:41-46).

Many people have taught this passage of Scripture as meaning that there will be actual nations that are considered goat nations and actual nations that are considered sheep nations. This isn't really a wrong concept, but it is wrong as far as personal judgment is concerned. You are not judged based on what your nation does. You're judged based on what you do, personally. You may be part of a nation that excludes God, but you follow Him wholeheartedly. Or you may be part of a nation that proclaims Jesus as Lord, but you do not follow Him. In either case, you're judged based on what you do, not what your nation does.

This passage regarding the sheep and the goats is referencing the great divide in the world. Goats are easy to spot in the world. When the goats are in the church, it's a little more difficult to spot them until they mature. You can reference the Parable of the Wheat and the Tares to understand that better.

The sheep are the ones who are the true Bride of Christ. They listen to His voice and follow Him. They are filled with His Spirit and love Him. Their love and devotion are played out through their faith. Their faith has been tested and found to be of the Spirit of Christ. Their works have come through the fire of testing because what they do has been born out of love for Jesus and faith in Him.

The religious who do not really love Jesus proclaim Him in name only. They are religious, and they do not follow His Spirit because they do not operate in faith. They are goats, who say they believe, but are liars. This is what it means to take the name of the Lord in vain: to say you bear His name, but you do not do what He does. They will be separated from the sheep and thrown into the fire. Notice too, that this shows the evil ones are removed, but the righteous remain. A rapture is simply not taught by Jesus.

The goats and sheep parable taught by Jesus is very simple. You will do works according to what you believe. If you believe Jesus, your faith will act accordingly, and you will be judged as a sheep. If Jesus is not your Lord, whether you're in the world or in the church, you will act accordingly, and you will be judged as a goat.

Jesus will come for a perfect bride, who is unblemished, without spot or wrinkle, a bride who is powerful and victorious, filled with faith and love. He's coming for a Bride who has been tested, tried, and proved faithful. He's coming for a Bride who has made Him the Head and is therefore in submission to Him. He is coming for a bride who is pure, and who is like Him and expresses faith through love. These are the days in which Jesus is building His church.

The Lord would like us to understand the times we are living in, and there are many Scriptures that point to the necessity of believers understanding the times they live in. However, there is one Scripture that seems to say we can't know that information. It is Acts 1:6-7.

> **Therefore, when they had come together, they asked Him, saying, "Lord, will You at this time restore the kingdom to Israel?" And He said to them, "It is not for you to know times or seasons which the Father has put in His own authority."**

Because of these two verses, some people think they are not allowed to know the season that we're in. However, that is not what Jesus is saying. The word translated "season" in the above verses is the word "kairos," and it means: opportune time, set time, appointed time, due time, definitive time, seasonable time, proper time for action. (Strong's #2540) Jesus meant we cannot know the appointed time of His return. We can understand the season or the times we're in, and we should, but we cannot know the exact date of His return.

For example, Jesus tells us that if we looked at a fig tree, we could tell what season it was based on what is going on with the fig tree (Matthew 24:32-33). Does it have leaves? Is it bearing figs? Even so, we should be able to look around us and see what time frame we're in based on what is happening around us. Is the world system being judged? Are the wheat and tares at the point of maturity where the tares would be taken out? Have some of the prophetic words Jesus prophesied come to pass? Looking at these things with the Holy Spirit gives us an idea where we are prophetically.

> But concerning the times and the seasons, brethren, you have no need that I should write to you. For you yourselves know perfectly that the day of the Lord so comes as a thief in the night. For when they say, "Peace and safety!" then sudden destruction comes upon them, as labor pains upon a pregnant woman. And they shall not escape. But you, brethren, are not in darkness, so that this Day should overtake you as a thief. You are all sons of light and sons of the day. We are not of the night nor of the darkness. Therefore let us not sleep, as others do, but let us watch and be sober. (1 Thessalonians 5:1-6)

Paul reiterates that we cannot know the exact date of the Lord's return, but that we ought to be watchful, meaning live in such a way as to ready ourselves for the fullness of His Kingdom at His return. This means that we walk in faith, listening to and obeying the Holy Spirit as we beat down the gates of hell. It means that we walk in love. We do not operate in accordance with the spirit of the world's system anymore. It also means that we understand who we are in Christ and who He is in us. We're not of those who are disobedient and will perish, but of those who are the righteousness of God in Christ, and who forever live to proclaim Him King. He is Lord of lords and King of kings!

Understanding the times we live in, while being unaware of the exact date of Jesus' return, causes us to operate in faith. Father always wants to bring us into more faith. He purposely doesn't reveal everything to us so that we must choose to operate in faith, even when we don't understand. Will we believe Him, or won't we?

The Bride of Christ will submit to the Holy Spirit and believe! And it's by the Holy Spirit we can understand the seasons we're living in, even if we don't know the exact date on which something will happen.

We can also look at prophecies that have come to pass. We know that Jerusalem was conquered by Rome, the temple was destroyed, and the Christians fled to the mountains (Luke 21:6, 20). There have also been other prophecies of Jesus' that have come to pass. For one, Jesus prophesied that the Jews would be killed and sent into exile (Luke 21:24 **"And they will fall by the edge of the sword, and be led away captive into all nations. And Jerusalem will be trampled by the Gentiles until the times of the Gentiles are fulfilled."**) This prophecy was fulfilled in 70 AD when the Romans defeated the Jews and destroyed Jerusalem and the temple, as well as killing a great number of Jews. They then forced nearly 100,000 people into exile. Josephus (a Jewish historian who saw what happened first-hand), writes, 'Now the number of those that were carried captive during this whole war was collected to be ninety-seven thousand." *(The Wars of the Jews, Book VI, Chapter 9)*

Additionally, Jesus prophesied that there would be false messiahs. Mark 13:5-6 reads, **"And Jesus answering them, began to say: 'Take heed that no one deceives you. For many will come in My name, saying, "I am He," and will deceive many.'"** Since Jesus ascended to heaven, there have been many people who have claimed to be the Messiah or have claimed that following them was the only way to heaven. Every one of them has been false.

And then there is the prophecy that there would be wars, rumors of war, earthquakes, pestilences, and famines. Have you noticed that this has happened pretty much continually since Jesus spoke it, and continues to happen to this day? We see famines in various parts of the world, there are earthquakes and threats of them, there are wars going on somewhere all the time, and still more rumors of them that we are told will wipe mankind off the planet. However, this does not indicate the end, but simply points to the time that the end is still to come.

Another prophecy is that the followers of Jesus would be persecuted, they would be betrayed and hated by their own, false prophets would rise up, and love would grow cold. This started happening immediately after the outpouring of the Holy Spirit. People accused the newly Spirit-filled church of being drunk as they mocked and ridiculed them. Shortly thereafter, James the brother of John was put to death, the church was persecuted and scattered, Stephen was martyred, Peter and John were put in prison, and much more. This persecution has continued to this day wherever the Spirit of the Lord is present.

Paul addresses this in 2 Timothy 3:1-9.

> But know this, that in the last days perilous times will come: For men will be lovers of themselves, lovers of money, boasters, proud, blasphemers, disobedient to parents, unthankful, unholy, unloving, unforgiving, slanderers, without self-control, brutal, despisers of good, traitors, headstrong, haughty, lovers of pleasure rather than lovers of God, having a form of godliness but denying its power. And from such people turn away! For of this sort are those who creep into households and make captives of gullible women loaded down with sins, led away by various lusts, always learning and never able to come to the knowledge of the truth. Now as Jannes and Jambres resisted Moses, so do these also resist the truth: men of corrupt minds, disapproved concerning the faith; but they will progress no further, for their folly will be manifest to all, as theirs also was.

He discusses perilous times that will come where men will be lovers of themselves and do all sorts of evil. However, he notes that their folly will become evident to all, which is exactly what Jesus was describing in the parable of the Wheat and the Tares when He says they will mature together. You can tell what something is really made of when it matures. These false prophets and false believers will be shown for who they are as well. And this sign too is happening right now.

All of these signs that Jesus said would point to the time of the end are either happening now or have happened in the past. There are some that have yet to occur, but the meaning of these will become clear in days to come because as the angel told Daniel, at the time of the end the wicked would not understand, but the wise would understand. It is through the Spirit of Christ that we understand the deep things of God. He gives us the revelation of Jesus Christ, and He will continue to reveal things as time goes on.

CHAPTER 6

THE BOOK OF REVELATION – THE BEGINNING

T he Revelation of Jesus Christ, which God gave Him to show His servants – things which must shortly take place. And He sent and signified it by His angel to His servant John, who bore witness to the word of God, and to the testimony of Jesus Christ, to all things that he saw. Blessed is he who reads and those who hear the words of this prophecy, and keep those things which are written in it; for the time is near. (Revelation 1:1-3)

First of all, the book of Revelation is the Revelation of Jesus Christ. It is not the revelation of the antichrist or the revelation of evil. Jesus is revealed as the Lamb who was slain and has been given the authority and power to judge. He is revealed as the righteous Judge who holds the iron scepter in His hand.

Throughout the Revelation of Jesus Christ, He reveals Himself in many ways. He declares,

"I am the Alpha and the Omega, the Beginning and the End, who is and who was and who is to come, the Almighty." (1:8)
"I am the Alpha and the Omega, the First and the Last." (1:11)
"I am the First and the Last." (1:17)
"I am He who lives, and was dead, and behold, I am alive forevermore. And I have the keys of Hades and of Death." (1:18)
[I Am] "… He who holds the seven stars in His right hand, who walks in the midst of the golden lampstands…" (2:1)

[I Am] "… the First and the Last, who was dead, and came to life…" (2:8)

[I Am] "… He who has the sharp two-edged sword…" (2:12)

[I Am] "… the Son of God, who has eyes like a flame of fire, and His feet like fine brass…" (2:18)

[I Am] "… He who has the seven Spirits of God and the seven stars…" (3:1)

[I Am] "… He who is holy, He who is true, He who has the key of David, He who opens and no one shuts, and shuts and no one opens…" (3:7)

[I Am] ".. the Amen, the Faithful and True Witness, the Beginning of the Creation of God…" (3:14)

[I Am] "… the Alpha and the Omega, the Beginning and the End, the First and the Last." (22:13)

[I Am] "… the Root and the Offspring of David, the Bright and Morning Star." (22:16)

Not only does Jesus call Himself these things, but He appears as a Lamb and as a Warrior, and others speak of Him saying things like,

"… the Lion of the tribe of Judah, the Root of David…" (5:5)

"… The One who is and who was and who is to come…" (11:17)

"… Lord God Almighty… King of the saints…" (15:3)

"… Lord God Omnipotent…" (19:6)

"… Faithful and True…" (19:11)

"… The Word of God…" (19:13)

"… King of kings and Lord of lords…" (19:16)

Secondly, the Revelation of Jesus Christ is "signified," meaning it is visionary, dream-like, using symbols or signs; it is prophetic. The book of Revelation is not straight-forward prose. Instead, you can impress on someone's senses better when something is shown and felt, rather than just spoken. The more senses that are involved, the better a thing is understood and remembered.

For example, my teen-age daughter had a dream that was rather frightening in some aspects and extremely vivid. The Holy Spirit told us He gave her a dramatic dream because it was something He really wanted her to remember, and He didn't want her to dismiss the message. The Revelation of Jesus Christ is also very dramatic, and because of it, very memorable. We do not just have words, but we have images that represent Jesus, world systems, rulers, and principalities, among other things.

Yet, through all of this, we must keep in mind that Revelation is revealing Jesus. He always was – He is – He always will be. He's the Creator. He's the rightful Judge. He's the Lamb slain before the foundation of the world. He is the Son born in Revelation 12, He's King of kings and Lord of lords in Revelation 19, and He's coming again in Revelation 22. Therefore, the overreaching theme of Revelation for us must be, "**The kingdoms of this world have become the kingdoms of our Lord and of His Christ, and He shall reign forever and ever!**" (Revelation 11:15)

Throughout the Revelation of Jesus Christ, John saw past, present, and future events (Revelation 1:9). It seems that many people miss this because they seem to think that everything should happen in a sequential manner. In other words, all the plagues must happen in order, and each successive chapter follows the previous chapter in order on a timeline, etc. However, this is not true.

The book of Revelation is not written linearly, but prophetically. This means that what we are reading is not happening in sequential order. Time was made for man, but God is outside of time. Therefore, when a prophet or in this case, an apostle, sees what is happening in Heaven, it can be difficult to translate that into a world where there is time.

The Lord said in a prophetic word on September 10, 2021,

"… the minutes, hours, days, and years are for men. The times, seasons, epochs, and eons are the Lord's. Therefore, I have made time for men, but My kingdom stands forever and is not dependent on time. My Prophets look into the things of the kingdom. They see things that I have set in motion. I tell them when I am about to do a thing. They 'translate' what they see and hear from My Kingdom and bring it to men. This 'translation' is difficult for them because of the transition from the eternal to the temporal." (*God's Prophetic Timing*)

He went on to say,

"When I speak to My Prophets, and when they prophesy about an event in the future, I have taken them out of their time paradigm and then placed them back into it in a different moment. They view the event, and then go back to where they left off. For this reason, it is difficult for them to time-stamp a future event unless I tell them, they see something which has a date on it, or some other means by which time can be evaluated. They travel through time in the Spirit, and it only takes an instant to happen." (*Time & the Prophetic*, October 24, 2022)

When we read Revelation, or any prophetic vision or word, we have to resist the urge to make it fit into a preconceived timeline. John saw the fall of Satan, the birth of Christ, the return of Christ, and everything in between in a very mixed-up order. He was seeing visions outside of time. It's the same as when the Scriptures declare that Jesus was the Lamb slain from the foundation of the world. On earth, we put the sacrifice of Christ into a timeline, but God says it was done before we ever saw it happen.

Revelation is written prophetically, not sequentially. It can only be interpreted then by the Spirit of Prophecy, who brings us revelation into the mysteries of God (1 Corinthians 2).

Knowing this, then, there are many things in Revelation that have already happened. We'll start with the seven churches mentioned in Revelation 1-3.

The seven churches that John wrote to in Revelation did actually exist. They were located in what we would call Asia Minor, or what is modern-day Turkey. The messages given for each church were specific for those churches, and yet like most prophetic words in Scripture, the Holy Spirit can use the same prophetic word multiple times for different circumstances. Take Isaiah 45:1-3 as an example. It reads,

> "Thus says the LORD to His anointed,
> To Cyrus, whose right hand I have held –
> To subdue nations before him
> And loose the armor of kings,
> To open before him the double doors,
> So that the gates will not be shut;
> I will go before you
> And make the crooked places straight;
> I will break in pieces the gates of bronze
> And cut the bars of iron.
> I will give you the treasures of darkness
> And hidden riches in secret places,
> That you may know that I, the LORD,
> Who call you by your name,
> Am the God of Israel."

The Lord used this prophecy about King Cyrus during the time of President Donald J. Trump, the 45th president, to prophecy the things that President Trump would accomplish. Notably the chapter is number 45, as is the President. This is one example, but the Lord does it all the time. The Holy Spirit inspired the Scriptures, and He's the one who can say what they mean at any given time.

The Lord said on August 24, 2021,

"The Father has set times and seasons for all things. He is sovereign, and there is no other. Yet in His love and mercy, He has desired to partner with men. He wants to partner through His Spirit who will lead you into all truth. On this day, He desires to show you how to understand the times you live in and yes, the end times also. He wants you to see the Scriptures that declare and predict the appearance of Jesus. He is simply asking - did the scholars know when He would appear? Or where? Or in what manner He would appear? I say, No! And yet in the year 2021, the scholars again think they can figure it all out. With great pride they point out how the Prophets are all wrong because what they say doesn't somehow line up with what they have figured out, or the signs that they have decided mean something. You must decide what to believe: words on a page, or My Spirit whose words will line up with the Scriptures. Amen." (*God's Prophetic Timing*)

In other words, we listen to the Holy Spirit, and He will confirm in Scripture what He says. We do not get to figure it out on our own.

Taking this into consideration, there were many churches in the time that Revelation was written. Each city that had born-again, Spirit-filled believers had a church in it. Yet, Jesus told John to write the seven letters to seven specific churches in Asia, even though these letters would end up being read by almost all the other believers living then and living later in history.

The individual details given to each church were specific for that particular church at that particular time. However, at times the Holy Spirit will use parts of these words to the seven churches as praises or admonitions to His people who are currently on the earth, even though these words have come to pass already.

To the church in Ephesus, Jesus says that they have persevered, have patience, and have labored for His name's sake. But He reprimands them for leaving their first love. It's not too hard to see that the Holy Spirit could reprimand any one of us who work for Him, but afterward start to drift away from loving Him. He's not looking for slaves, but sons. A son works out of love. A slave works out of duty. Hence, this word to the Ephesians can be used over and over as many times as Jesus chooses.

Jesus then tells the church in Smyrna He knows their works, tribulation, and poverty, and He warns them that they will be tested, face tribulation and be thrown in prison. And yet He encourages them to stay faithful. Again, the Holy Spirit can bring parts of this word to His people all around the world who face similar circumstances as the church in Smyrna, even though this church was an actual church, and this was a literal word from Jesus to that church. Additionally, the persecution that came through Emperor Diocletian lasted ten years, which we'll read about when we discuss the fifth seal.

After this, Jesus tells the church in Thyatira,

> **"I know your works, love, service, faith, and your patience... Nevertheless I have a few things against you, because you allow that woman Jezebel, who calls herself a prophetess, to teach and seduce My servants to commit sexual immorality and eat things sacrificed to idols."** (Revelation 2:19-20)

While these exact circumstances may not occur in another church in history, it is true that we can be loving, faithful, and patient, working diligently to spread the gospel, and still be soft on sin. Sometimes the desire to love people causes us to allow something into our fellowship that shouldn't be there. We call it "Nice Theology." Being nice doesn't mean patting people on the back all the way to hell. So, just like Jesus corrected the church in Thyatira, He may use these Scriptures again to correct another part of His church today, but that does not mean that this has not already happened.

After Thyatira, Jesus rebukes the church in Sardis for acting like they are alive, but actually they are dead. Sounds like religion. We've had many words given to the church regarding religion. Doing works outside the leading of and submission to the Holy Spirit will not get us anywhere, even if those works look good on the outside. And yet, just like in the churches today, there was a remnant in Sardis who did not defile their garments (Revelation 3:4).

The church in Philadelphia follows Sardis and is seemingly the polar opposite. This church is commended for persevering and promised great rewards. Though this was a literal church at the time, the Holy Spirit can bring parts of these same words and use them again for other churches throughout the earth at any time He desires to encourage and strengthen the body of Christ.

Lastly, the church in Laodicea is rebuked for being lukewarm. This is perhaps the most well-known church because it is the last one listed, and so for many years people have thought it was representative of the current church. It may be representative of the institutional church, but it is definitely not representative of the true church of Jesus Christ. His church loves Him and follows Him. His church lays her life down for His name. His church is like Him. Praise God!

Besides the seven churches, there are also other events throughout Revelation that have come to pass since John saw them, or were already in the past when they were shown to John. For example, Revelation 4 shows the Lord on His throne with the creatures, saints, and angels worshiping Him. This is something that had been going on before John saw it, was going on when John saw it, and continues to go on today. Heaven is timeless, and this is something that occurs continually.

In Revelation 5, John witnesses Jesus as the sacrificial Lamb who defeated sin, sickness, and death. As such, He is the One throughout Revelation who has been found worthy to judge. Jesus said in Matthew 10:34, **"Do not think that I came to bring peace on earth. I did not come to bring peace but a sword."** Jesus goes on to say that He is the dividing line between those who choose to follow God and those who do not. Throughout His judgments in Revelation, He is dividing between those who are His and those who are not.

We will begin the judgments in the next chapter.

CHAPTER 7

THE SEVEN SEALS & THE SEVEN TRUMPETS

————————◆‣◈‣‣◆————————

Revelation 6 describes six of the seven seals that Jesus, the Lamb, opens.

> Now I saw when the Lamb opened one of the seals; and I heard one of the four living creatures saying with a voice like thunder, "Come and see." And I looked, and behold, a white horse. He who sat on it had a bow; and a crown was given to him, and he went out conquering and to conquer. (Revelation 6:1-2)

The first seal reveals the conquering of Israel, which happened between 64 AD and 70 AD, culminating in the destruction of the holy city, the temple, and its people. Those who did not perish were brought into captivity. The rider and the horse in this first seal represent Rome. The crown given to the rider represents the Lord's approval and shows that Rome was doing what they did out of what He had given them. He had given permission for them to conquer because Israel did not recognize the Messiah when He came.

This is just as Jesus prophesied in Luke 19:41-44.

> Now as He drew near, He saw the city and wept over it, saying, "If you had known, even you, especially in this your day, the things that make for your peace! But now they are hidden from your eyes. For days will come upon you when your enemies will build an embankment around you, surround you and close you in on every side, and level you, and your children within you, to the ground; and they will not leave in you one stone upon another, because you did not know the time of your visitation."

This is why Jesus told His followers to leave when they saw the armies coming against Jerusalem, because His people were not to be under this judgment.

After this came the second seal.

> When he opened the second seal, I heard the second living creature saying, "Come and see." Another horse, fiery red, went out. And it was granted to the one who sat on it to take peace from the earth, and that people should kill one another; and there was given to him a great sword. (Revelation 6:3-4)

The second seal begins the judgment on Rome and the world system it represents. It reveals the removal of peace, culminating in people killing one another. Between 180-235 AD, Rome fought civil wars as emperors came and went. These civil wars within the nation led to the third seal.

> When He opened the third seal, I heard the third living creature say, "Come and see." So I looked, and behold, a black horse, and he who sat on it had a pair of scales in his hand. And I heard a voice in the midst of the four living creatures saying, "A quart of wheat for a denarius, and three quarts of barley for a denarius; and do not harm the oil and the wine." (Revelation 6:5-6)

The third seal in Revelation 6 reveals a black horse who brings with it economic crisis. There have been many economic downturns throughout history, but this seal is referencing the hyperinflation due to the devaluation of Roman coins in Rome between 235-249 AD. Roman citizens were heavily taxed due to the immense wars fought by the military. Taxes could be paid in grain, oil, and wine. This heavy taxation led to famine.

> When he opened the fourth seal, I heard the voice of the fourth living creature saying, "Come and see." So I looked, and behold,

a pale horse. And the name of him who sat on it was Death, and Hades followed with him. And power was given to them over a fourth of the earth, to kill with sword, with hunger, with death, and by the beasts of the earth. (Revelation 6:7-8)

The fourth seal occurred during 249-262 AD when after Rome experienced civil wars and famine, they then fell into disease, causing much death. At one point, it was reported that 5,000 people were dying per day. The famine from the third seal was still raging, and the in-fighting from the second seal was still happening. Hence, sword, hunger, and death, as the seal indicates.

When He opened the fifth seal, I saw under the altar the souls of those who had been slain for the word of God and for the testimony which they held. And they cried with a loud voice, saying, "How long, O Lord, holy and true, until You judge and avenge our blood on those who dwell on the earth?" Then a white robe was given to each of them; and it was said to them that they should rest a little while longer, until both the number of their fellow servants and their brethren, who would be killed as they were, was completed. (Revelation 6:9-11)

The fifth seal began around 303 AD and ended in 313 AD. During this period the persecution of Christians intensified to an extent never before seen in Rome. In 303, Emperor Diocletian

"overturned the laws passed in 260 (which protected Christians) and issued edicts outlawing the faith and compelling all citizens to worship and sacrifice to the "old gods" of Rome (Jews were exempted). Those who did not were subject to imprisonment or even execution. This attack was much more comprehensive than earlier ones. Nero, for example, while he executed Christians, restricted his attacks to Rome only. The Diocletianic Persecution was empire-wide... By the summer of 303, a second edict was published ordering the imprisonment of all clergy. The next year another edict was issued requiring all citizens to make their sacrifices to the gods publicly, and if they refused, they were to be executed." (Great Persecution (303-313) - HistoriaRex.com)

It's interesting that Jesus told the church in Smyrna they would have tribulation for 10 days, and this incredibly intense period lasted for 10 years.

I looked when He opened the sixth seal, and behold, there was a great earthquake; and the sun became black as sackcloth of hair, and the moon became like blood. And the stars of heaven fell to the earth, as when a fig tree drops its late figs when it is shaken by a mighty wind. Then the sky receded as a scroll when it is rolled up, and every mountain and island was moved out of its place. And the kings of the earth, the great men, the rich men, the commanders, the mighty men, every slave and every free man, hid themselves in the caves and in the rocks of the mountains, and said to the mountains and rocks, "Fall on us and hide us from the face of Him who sits on the throne and from the wrath of the Lamb! For the great day of His wrath has come, and who is able to stand?" (Revelation 6:12-17)

The sixth seal depicting an earthquake, stars falling, the sky receding, and people hiding themselves from the wrath of God, is a vision of the fall of the heathen Roman Empire. This judgment against Rome occurred during the reign of Constantine, a convert to Christianity. He ended the persecution against Christians, and throughout his reign and that of Theodosius I, the paganism of Rome was mostly demolished, and some of the previous persecutors of believers supposedly repented. Additionally, it is reported that under Constantine, about half of Rome converted to Christianity. The demolition of pagan Rome and all her gods was like stars falling from heaven and the sky receding like a scroll. The empire still stood, but it was no longer predominately pagan. The fall of the pagan Roman Empire was a very dramatic event in history.

Through these seals, Jesus showed the Church what was to come, revealing His judgments. At our point in history, we see these six seals as having already happened.

After the first six seals, John sees four angels holding back the wind until the servants of God receive His seal. It then goes into a multitude who have come out of tribulation. This is a depiction of the church of Jesus Christ. The number 144,000 divisible by 12 into 12,000 is a perfect cube. It is the Spirit-filled church, and those who have endured tribulation, not just as physical martyrs, but those who stand in faith, stand before the throne in the Spirit, and will receive a great reward because they have died to self. This part of the Revelation of Jesus Christ has been happening since the Spirit was first poured out. From every generation there have been those who have come out of tribulation with faith. Jesus is building His church. We are living stones built on the foundation of the apostles and prophets with Jesus Christ as the Chief Cornerstone. And yet, the building is not complete until the end.

After the vision of the perfect church, John sees the 7th seal be opened wherein he witnesses the prayers of the saints mixed with the smoke of incense in Heaven. Then an angel sounds the first trumpet, which is hail and fire with blood and a third of the vegetation and trees burned up. Trumpets in Scripture are usually a call to battle. These trumpets indicate wars.

The first angel sounded: And hail and fire followed, mingled with blood, and they were thrown to the earth. And a third of the trees were burned up, and all green grass was burned up. (Revelation 8:7)

The First Trumpet came when the Visigoths attacked the Roman Empire between 400 – 410 AD after the death of Emperor Theodosius I. Led by Alaric, the Goths represent hail from the North. The fire represents their scorched earth policy, and the blood is representative of the numerous deaths caused by this invasion and sacking of Rome.

> **Then the second angel sounded: And something like a great mountain burning with fire was thrown into the sea, and a third of the sea became blood. And a third of the living creatures in the sea died, and a third of the ships were destroyed. (Revelation 8:8-9)**

The Second Trumpet was a battle of the seas, fulfilled by the great nation (a mountain) of Vandals led by Genseric, who attacked the Mediterranean coastlands, as well as the islands from 425-470 AD. Again, there was much blood spilled in this war.

> **Then the third angel sounded: And a great star fell from heaven, burning like a torch, and it fell on a third of the rivers and on the springs of water. The name of the star is Wormwood. A third of the waters became wormwood, and many men died from the water, because it was made bitter. (Revelation 8:10-11)**

The Third Trumpet released a great star called Wormwood, which made the waters bitter. This great star was Attila the Hun, who was called "the scourge of God." It is known that Attila fought his major battles on rivers. In fact, he came from the area around a river in Illyricum, which is called Wormwood in Greek ("Apsynthos"). He would lure Roman armies into crossing the rivers, and as they crossed, the Huns would attack. It is estimated that 300,000 men were left dead in the source of the Danube, Rhine, and Po rivers, which fed into over 40 rivers that covered 1/3 of the Roman Empire, their dead, rotting bodies making the water bitter. Hence this trumpet blast has been fulfilled.

> **Then the fourth angel sounded. And a third of the sun was struck, a third of the moon, and a third of the stars, so that a third of them were darkened. A third of the day did not shine, and likewise the night. And I looked, and I heard an angel flying through the midst of heaven, saying with a loud voice, "Woe, woe, woe to the inhabitants of the earth, because of the remaining blasts of the trumpet of the three angels who are about to sound!"** (Revelation 8:12-13)

The Fourth Trumpet depicts a third of the sun, moon, and stars darkened. We know from Genesis 37:9 that Joseph dreamed his father, mother, and brothers were represented by the sun, moon, and stars. The sun, moon, and stars are symbolic of those in authority and of a kingdom. The fourth trumpet represents the downfall of Roman leadership when Romulus Augustalus, the last Roman Emperor of the West, was captured in 476 AD by the Heruli, who were led by Odoacer. Augustalus was the top leader of one third of the Roman Empire. He would be the sun in this case. The lesser leaders, the moon and stars, represent the lesser Roman leaders in the hierarchy of power. These first four trumpets ended the Roman Empire, leaving behind only the Eastern part of the Empire, which became known as the Byzantine Empire.

> **Then the fifth angel sounded: And I saw a star fallen from heaven to the earth. To him was given the key to the bottomless pit ... Then out of the smoke locusts came upon the earth. And to them was given power, as the scorpions of the earth have power. They were commanded not to harm the grass of the earth, or any green thing, or any tree, but only those men who do not have the seal of God on their foreheads. And they were not given authority to kill**

them, but to torment them for five months. Their torment was like the torment of a scorpion when it strikes a man. In those days men will seek death and will not find it; they will desire to die, and death will flee from them. The shape of the locusts was like horses prepared for battle. On their heads were crowns of something like gold, and their faces were like the faces of men. They had hair like women's hair, and their teeth were like lions' teeth. And they had breastplates of iron, and the sound of their wings was like the sound of chariots with many horses running into battle. They had tails like scorpions, and there were stings in their tails. Their power was to hurt men five months. And they had as king over them the angel of the bottomless pit, whose name in Hebrew is Abaddon, but in Greek he has the name Apollyon. (Revelation 9:1-11)

The Fifth Trumpet begins the woes. After the west was conquered, Christianity in the eastern Roman Empire became decidedly institutionalized by the Catholic church. This was paganism mixed with Christianity, with a man (the pope) put at the head of the church. Emperor Constantine moved the capital of Rome to Constantinople in 313 AD, and later the Christian religion became the official religion of Rome.

David and Tim Barton record the following in their book *The American Story, the Beginnings*:

... [I]n 390 AD... Emperor Theodosius I unilaterally assumed control of the Church and assimilated it into the State, decreeing Christianity as the official religion of the empire and declaring all other religions illegal ... Thereafter, State leaders often made themselves head of the Christian Church, with church officials answering to government authorities and enforcing any religious doctrines the civil leaders decreed. This arrangement became known as a State-established church. (p. 33)

This way of running a nation is not in the best interest of the people. The Church should influence the government, not the other way around. Pretty soon, only Catholics were recognized as Christians. Much persecution of true believers and those of other faiths came via the hands of the Roman Catholic Church.

At the same time, much persecution against anyone calling themselves "Christians" came at the hands of the Muslims, who attacked the Eastern Empire for 150 years, after Mohammed died in 632 AD until the Treaty of Constantinople was signed in 782, which fulfills the five month prophecy when one day equals one year (5 months x 30 days = 150 years). The Muslim religion is demonic in nature, and the description of the locusts (who literally come out for five months between April and September) fits the Muslims in imagery. For example, they rode horses very well, they wore turbans that looked like crowns, they had long hair like women, but faces covered in beards, like men, and they wore breastplates. They also shot arrows behind or before them as they rode, hence the stinging in the tails of the scorpions.

During the Fifth Trumpet, the Muslims attacked Constantinople, but they failed to take it, only tormenting the people instead of killing them. However, the Sixth Trumpet did lead to the downfall of the rest of what was left of the Roman Empire, including Constantinople. Judgment came to the eastern empire through the Muslims.

Then the sixth angel sounded: And I heard a voice from the four horns of the golden altar which is before God, saying to the sixth angel who had the trumpet, "Release the four angels who are bound at the great river Euphrates." So the four angels who had been prepared for the hour and day and month and year were

released to kill a third of mankind. Now the number of the army of the horsemen was two hundred million; I heard the number of them. And thus I saw the horses in the vision: those who sat on them had breastplates of fiery red, hyacinth blue, and sulfur yellow; and the heads of the horses were like the heads of lions; and out of their mouths came fire, smoke, and brimstone. By these three plagues a third of mankind was killed – by the fire and the smoke and the brimstone which came out of their mouths. For their power is in their mouth and in their tails; for their tails are like serpents, having heads; and with them they do harm. (Revelation 9:13-19)

As stated, the Sixth Trumpet is describing the Turkish Empire defeating the rest of the Roman Empire.

Revelation 9:16 reads, "Now the number of the army of the horsemen was two hundred million; I heard the number of them." This is a very poor translation. What is translated "hundred million" actually means "ten thousand" or "innumerable multitude." The Turks organized their armies into units of ten thousand. The Turks also wore uniforms of red, blue, and yellow, and the leader who led them across the Euphrates River was known as the "Valiant Lion." His given name was Alp Arsion. Additionally, the Turks wore horse tails on their hats, used gunpowder and cannons in battle, having to light the tail of the cannon, with the explosion coming out of its "mouth." Constantinople (built on 7 hills), which was renamed Istanbul, fell because of this artillery. The newly established Istanbul ended the sixth trumpet in 1543.

After the defeat of the Roman Empire in 1543, something much more insidious rose to power, something claiming to be for Jesus, but was not.

Under the authority of the Roman Catholic Church, came the Jesuits in 1540. Their goal at first was to bring Protestants back under the rule of the Roman Catholic Church. However, they are, and have been, comprised of the wealthy families (Rothschilds, Morgans, Rockefellers, etc.) who rule the monetary system. The Jesuits work through the following organizations: the Illuminati, the Council on Foreign Relations, the International Bankers, the Mafia (the criminal arm of the Vatican), the Club of Rome, the Opus Dei, the Masons, and the New Age Movement. There are more, but these are the prominent organizations they are involved in, some of which look good on the outside, but are evil. We will refer to the Jesuits in power as Luciferians because they worship Satan, and are empowered by that serpent.

One article states:

> The Society of Jesus, more commonly referred to as the Jesuits, are the armed militia of the Roman Catholic Church. They were sanctioned in 1540 by Pope Paul III with one mandate: to defeat Protestantism and regain worldwide Papal rule. To achieve this monumental task, they employ ever-adapting methods of pseudo-education, social programs, infiltration, and all wickedness that could possibly be conceived. Needless to say, they are achieving great success in their mission, which is climaxing with the present pope, Pope Francis…
> (https://prepareforchange.net/2019/11/05/10-facts-you-must-know-about-the-jesuits/)

Over the years, the Jesuits have infiltrated every mountain of influence in society and have set up their Luciferian world order on the tops of each mountain. The following excerpts will give you an example of what the Jesuits are doing.

Obviously, the Jesuits were not expelled from many nations (even Catholic nations) because of their educational or charity work. They were expelled for engaging in and carrying out subversive political plots against humanity to advance their own cause.

> "Between 1555 and 1931 the Society of Jesus [i.e., the Jesuit Order] was expelled from at least 83 countries, city states and cities, for engaging in political intrigue and subversion plots against the welfare of the State, according to the records of a Jesuit priest of repute [i.e., Thomas J. Campbell]. Practically every instance of expulsion was for political intrigue, political infiltration, political subversion, and inciting to political insurrection."

> The Jesuits are known for their deception, spying, infiltration, assassination, and revolution. They worked deep into the political field and plotted through politics throughout the world countries. (Source: "The Babington Plot", by J.E.C. Shepherd, p.12)

> When the Jesuits are expelled from a country, they simply change strategies and return to the country they were expelled from under a new disguise. The following sums up their operational strategy: "We came in like lambs and will rule like wolves. We shall be expelled like dogs and return like eagles." Source: Francesco Borgia, Third Jesuit Superior General. (https://prepareforchange. net/2019/11/05/10-facts-you-must-know-about-the-jesuits/)

An understanding of this part of history is necessary in order to move on from the trumpet prophecies to the prophecies of the bowls of wrath in Revelation 16.

For now, we will bring the focus back on Jesus and His plans for humanity. Psalm 2:1-5 reads,

Why do the nations rage
And the people plot a vain thing?

The kings of the earth have set themselves,
And the rulers take counsel together,
Against the LORD and against His Anointed, saying,
"Let us break Their bonds in pieces
And cast away Their cords from us."
He who sits in the heavens shall laugh;
The Lord shall hold them in derision.
Then He shall speak to them in His wrath,
And distress them in His deep displeasure…

Do you see what a vain thing it is to come against the Lord and His people? Jesus always wins. In fact, the Lord never even has thoughts of losing. So no matter what those who do the bidding of the evil one think up, they will never take the Lord by surprise or even come close to defeating Him.

As the Prophecy from March 8, 2022 entitled "Actors" says, the Lord always wins!

The Lord says that virtually all of the leaders of the world are actors. I couldn't imagine that! He continued … *"Yes, some of those who you suppose to be the elected leaders are really other people. Yes, truly actors! Others are not leaders. They merely act the part, but have been compromised through and through. They are acting the part of 'leader,' but they do not lead. They merely follow orders. They would do anything that they were ordered to do – start wars, murder their own people, even go nuclear. They are sold out totally to evil and they both know it, and actually embrace the evil one, and have decided to follow/obey the devil's minions in their cabal. Therefore, I, the LORD, Am telling you this My people so that you will not mourn the demise of these people who are in leadership and places of power over the nations. I Am also wants you to know that there are those who have not been compromised! There are even those who do My bidding who do not know Me! Therefore, do not give way to fear. I know the end from the beginning. I have NEVER been fooled, never been confused, never felt weak. I have never sat wringing My hands in worry AND I NEVER LOSE! My Anointed will step forward! The Trump card will be played. And those who deal in fear will become fearful! My justice WILL be served! ALL of this will come into play soon, very soon! So keep your eyes on My goodness and My promises of the good times to come! Do not bow My People! Do not fear! My Spirit is being poured out on anyone willing to carry Him! Ask for Him. You will not be denied! Amen!"*

Praise the LORD! He is so good!

CHAPTER 8

REVELATION CHAPTERS 12, 13, & 14

————————◆◂◂◆▸▸◆————————

For what does the Scripture say? "Abraham believed God, and it was accounted to him for righteousness." Now to him who works, the wages are not counted as grace but as debt... How then was it accounted? While he was circumcised or uncircumcised? Not while circumcised, but while uncircumcised. And he received the sign of circumcision... that he might be the father of all who believe, though they are uncircumcised... For the promise that he would be the heir of the world was not to Abraham or to his seed through the law, but through the righteousness of faith. For if those who are of the law are heirs, faith is made void and the promise made of no effect. (Romans 4:3-4, 10-14)

Through Abraham the nation of Israel came to be. Yet, Abraham is not only the father of the circumcised in the flesh, but also of those circumcised in the spirit. In Revelation 12, we see both of these facets at work.

Now a great sign appeared in heaven: a woman clothed with the sun, with the moon under her feet, and on her head a garland of twelve stars. Then being with child, she cried out in labor and in pain to give birth. And another sign appeared in heaven: behold, a great, fiery red dragon having seven heads and ten horns, and seven diadems on his heads. His tail drew a third of the stars of heaven and threw them to the earth. And the dragon stood before the woman who was ready to give birth, to devour her Child as soon as it was born. She bore a male Child who was to rule all nations with a rod of iron. And her Child was caught up to God and His throne ... And war broke out in heaven: Michael and his angels fought with the dragon; and the dragon and his angels fought, but they did not prevail, nor was a place found for them in heaven any longer. So the great dragon was cast out, that serpent of old, called the Devil and Satan, who deceives the whole world; he was cast to the earth, and his angels were cast out with him. Then I heard a loud voice saying in heaven, "Now salvation, and strength, and the kingdom of our God, and the power of His Christ have come, for the accuser of our brethren, who accused them before our God day and night, has been cast down. And they overcame him by the blood of the Lamb and by the word of their testimony, and they did not love their lives to the death ... And the dragon was enraged with the woman, and he went to make war with the rest of her offspring, who keep the commandments of God and have the testimony of Jesus Christ. (Revelation 12:1-5, 7-11, 17)

Natural Israel brings forth the Messiah – the woman clothed in the sun with the garland of 12 stars on her head. (Remember the depiction of Israel in Joseph's dream.) And yet, we can even say this is spiritual Israel because it is those with faith who were engaged in the work of bringing the Messiah, all the way from Jacob who covenanted with God in faith, to Mary and Joseph who operated in faith. As Jesus said to the woman at the well, "... [S]alvation is of the Jews."

The first Christians were Jews, who did not consider believing in Jesus to be in opposition to being a Jew. He is the Messiah the Jews were waiting for, so they still considered themselves Jews. As Jesus said to the church in Philadelphia, "Indeed I will make those of the synagogue of Satan, who say they are Jews and are not, but lie – indeed I will make them come and worship before your feet, and to know that I have loved you." (Revelation 3:9) In other words, a true Jew was one who worshiped Jesus, one who was of faith, like Abraham, not just someone who physically came from the seed of Abraham. Therefore, we see the enemy again attacking those who follow Jesus, or as it says in Revelation, those who **"keep the commandments of God and have the testimony of Jesus Christ."** (12:17)

The dragon in this chapter represents Satan, who tried to kill Jesus, but of course the LORD defeated death and the devil, and ascended into Heaven. After which, the enemy came after natural Israel and spiritual Israel to destroy them. Michael defeats the enemy, casting him out of heaven, even as those who believe and are empowered with the authority of Jesus take their stand in the earth. As Jesus said to the 72, **"I saw Satan fall like lightning from heaven. Behold, I give you the authority to trample on serpents and scorpions, and over all the power of the enemy, and nothing shall by any means hurt you."** (Luke 10:18-19)

John testifies that they overcame the enemy **"by the blood of the Lamb and by the word of their testimony,"** and by not loving their lives to the death (Revelation 12:11). This is true Christianity – victory in Jesus!

After Revelation 12, John records a vision not in chronological order, but evidently in the order he saw the visions of two beasts. Perhaps the most famous part of this vision is regarding the number 666.

> **Here is wisdom. Let him who has understanding calculate the number of the beast, for it is the number of a man: His number is 666.** (Revelation 13:18)

The first beast is the one whose name numerically is 666. John tells his readers to calculate the number of the beast, or as it says in verse 17, "the number of his name."

Calculating a number for a name is called "gematria." Using gematria, people would transform names into numbers by giving the letters numerical values. So, for example, there have been objects found in ancient Rome with graffiti written on them. It might say, "I love 542," instead of, "I love Aggripina," or something like that. Using gematria, a person could write in code, and it would require those who read what was written in code to have some knowledge about what's going on in the world or in that particular situation in order to translate the numbers into a name.

In John's case, he was writing the book of Revelation from the Island of Patmos. Evidently, he was imprisoned on Patmos by the Roman Emperor Domitian. As John wrote the vision he received, he used code for his own sake and those who would read the vision since Rome would not take kindly to what it would perceive as some form of insurrection against its rule. You could compare this to how in modern days those who oppose the globalist agenda and are awake to the truth have had to speak and write in code on various platforms whenever they mention the COVID injections, masks, stolen elections, and so much more that goes against the mainstream narrative. In our case, we may get censored or even jailed. In John's case, it could mean death for him or for the church who would receive the vision.

John's readers would have understood what he was doing. They were living in it. Therefore, it wouldn't be too difficult for the church to decipher that Nero Caesar transliterated into Hebrew is 666. (Transliterate means to take the characters of one alphabet and represent them in another. So, John wrote in Greek, but taking those letters and representing them in Hebrew, then Nero Caesar is 666.) Giving Nero a code name in Greek would have been too easy for the Romans to decipher. Giving it in Hebrew would have been safer.

For Nero to fit with 666, his title must be used. More specifically, if you take Nero's name and title in Greek, and transliterate it into Hebrew (קסר נרון), and then take the numerical value, it totals 666. Interestingly, it is said that both Domitian and Vespasian also equate to 666 when their title of Ceasar is used. Whether or not that is true, Nero, Domitian, and Vespasian, all had antichrist spirits. So when the Scriptures say that the beast was wounded and lived, Nero killed himself and yet the spirit behind him lived on in the emperors Domitian and Vespasian, the former being the one who imprisoned John.

God frequently speaks in visions. Jesus is wisdom, so He knows just how to speak and what to show us in every situation. It's no accident that He showed John a beast to represent someone that John should refrain from naming by name. In our case, He's shown the deep state as vermin, He's shown the Chinese Communist Party as a lizard, He's referenced the stealer of the White House as the "imposter," and so much more.

When Jesus prophesied that the temple would be torn down, it happened after Nero's death in the reign of Vespasian, who sent his son, Titus, to destroy Jerusalem. Titus did according to Vespasian's orders, and so thoroughly destroyed the temple that no rock was found on another. This prophecy of Jesus' actually happened.

Much of Revelation has also actually happened. In fact, some of it was history when John was seeing it, which is not unusual for a prophet to experience. Jesus Christ is the same yesterday, today, and forever, and He can show us yesterday, today, and forever if He so chooses. As Jesus said in Revelation 1:19, **"Write the things which** you have seen, and the things which are, and the things which will take place after this." In other words, Jesus is going to show John things from the past, present, and future in this vision. The antichrist spirit is one of those things that has happened and continues to happen.

John is the only one who writes about an antichrist in the Scriptures. He clearly indicates that there are many antichrists because antichrist is a spirit. Some of those who operate in the antichrist spirit are then considered an antichrist. The antichrist spirit has been inducing men and women throughout history to come against Christ, and this is the same spirit behind the Abomination of Desolation spoken of by Daniel the Prophet.

Daniel wrote that the abomination of desolation would stand in the holy place. Some have interpreted the holy place to be the temple in Jerusalem, but actually Jerusalem itself was considered holy. At least 11 times in Scripture Jerusalem is called the "holy city." Two examples include:

- **Then the devil took him to the holy city and set him on the pinnacle of the temple** (Matthew 4:5 ESV)
- **Seventy weeks are decreed about your people and your holy city.** (Daniel 9:24 ESV)

Therefore, it wasn't necessary that there needed to be an abomination in the temple itself. An abomination that makes desolate in the city would also fulfill the prophecy. To some extent Daniel's prophecy was fulfilled when Antiochus IV Epiphanes (he gave himself the surname "Epiphanes," which means "God made manifest") conquered Jerusalem, set up an altar to Zeus in the temple, and sacrificed a pig thereon. However, Jesus said that Daniel's prophecy had not been fulfilled yet, but that His disciples would see it be fulfilled. He said,

"Therefore when you see the 'abomination of desolation,' spoken of by Daniel the prophet, standing in the holy place" (whoever reads, let him understand), "then let those who are in Judea flee to the mountains. Let him who is on the housetop not go down to take anything out of his house. And let him who is in the field not go back to get his clothes." (Matthew 24:15-18)

Around 33-37 years after Jesus' prophesied the destruction of the temple, the surrounding of Jerusalem, and a great tribulation, his prophecy came to pass. Many of Jesus' disciples did see the abomination of desolation in the holy city, and in the temple itself.

The Jews would not allow idols into the holy city of Jerusalem. However, before the destruction of Jerusalem, Roman soldiers brought into the city their ensigns that included an eagle with an image of Caesar underneath it. Caesar claimed to be divine, and the Roman soldiers would worship daily the image of Caesar. Supposedly, the Jews entreated Pilate to take that "abomination of desolation" out of their Holy City and from the area surrounding their Holy Temple. (Carroll, B.H. *An Introduction of the English Bible,* p. 263-264, 1947.) The Jews actually referred to the ensign of the Roman army as an abomination of desolation.

Of course, the Romans didn't do as the Jews requested, but instead came with other armies, surrounded the city, tore down the wall, slaughtered the inhabitants, and burned down the temple, leaving no stone on another. The abomination that causes desolation had come, just as Jesus said it would. And behind it was the antichrist spirit.

It is interesting to note that Rome is built on seven hills, or mountains. Revelation 17:9 reads, **"Here is the mind which has wisdom: The seven heads are seven mountains on which the woman sits."** Here John is referencing the woman sitting on the beast system, with Rome as the beast. The head of the beast system, the emperor, would be operating in the same spirit as the system itself, which is the antichrist spirit. Therefore when the abomination of desolation was found in the holy place, the city of Jerusalem, it was inspired by the antichrist spirit. There is no abomination that causes desolation without it being inspired by an antichrist spirit. They are one and the same.

We discussed previously that Nero Caesar is the first beast from Revelation 13. His name is 666. The dragon (Satan) was behind the evil doings of Nero, and Nero in turn persecuted believers, and forced worship of demons. Romans had an ensign they worshiped that had an image of Caesar on it (worship the image of the beast), and Caesar was considered the ruler of the world. These things in Chapter 13 of Revelation have occurred.

Chapter 14 brings us to the 144,000 mentioned in Revelation Chapter 7. John writes,

> **Then I looked, and behold, a Lamb standing on Mount Zion, and with Him one hundred and forty-four thousand, having His Father's name written on their foreheads.** (Revelation 14:1)

The 144,000 with the Lamb represent a perfect cube, like the vision Ezekiel saw of a temple with perfect proportions. The Holy Spirit, or the presence of God, dwells in those who have been made new in Christ. Those in Christ are a perfect temple, represented by 12,000 from each tribe of Israel: perfection. The perfect church is also depicted in Revelation 21:9-27 where New Jerusalem's proportions are made up of twelves. The Bride of Christ is pictured as the new Holy City with Jesus as her temple.

Currently, this part of the vision is occurring. The Bride, or the New Jerusalem, represented by the perfect number of 144,000 will be complete when all of the harvest has come in. As the writer of Hebrews testifies, **"And all these, having obtained a good testimony** through faith, did not receive the promise, God having provided something better for us, that they should not be made perfect apart from us." (Hebrews 11:39-40)

It is also interesting to note that the church has Father's name written on her forehead. This is not a literal writing, just as it's not necessary to look for a literal mark on those who worship the beast or the antichrist spirit. The mark of the beast is fear, and the mark of the Lord is love. Father is always looking at our hearts. So, the mark on the forehead is indicative of what someone thinks or believes, and the mark on the hand is indicative of what someone does. We will act according to what we believe in our hearts. That's true faith, and for those in Christ, the mark of love will flow out of our hearts in acts of faith.

Revelation 14 ends with an image of the wrath of God poured out on the disobedient.

> Then another angel came out of the temple which is in heaven, he also having a sharp sickle. And another angel came out from the altar, who had power over fire, and he cried with a loud cry to him who had the sharp sickle, saying, "Thrust in your sharp sickle and gather the clusters of the vine of the earth, for her grapes are fully ripe." So the angel thrust his sickle into the earth and gathered the vine of the earth, and threw it into the great winepress of the wrath of God. And the winepress was trampled outside the city, and blood came out of the winepress, up to the horses' bridles, for one thousand six hundred furlongs. (Revelation 14:17-20)

Just like Jesus told us in the Parable of the Wheat and the Tares, the angels are the harvesters at the end of the age. Each judgment that Jesus brings has, and will, bring wrath on those who choose the worship of the devil over the worship of God. There is no in-between. As Paul writes, **"Do you not know that to whom you present** yourselves slaves to obey, you are that one's slaves whom you obey, whether of sin leading to death, or of obedience leading to righteousness?" (Romans 6:16)

For those of us in Christ, we are no longer a slave to sin, to death, or to the mark of the beast, which is fear. We are slaves to righteousness.

> **But God be thanked that though you were slaves of sin, yet you obeyed from the heart that form of doctrine to which you were delivered. And having been set free from sin, you became slaves of righteousness.** (Romans 6:17-18)

Speaking of the mark of the beast, we know that ultimately the mark of the beast is fear, and even though many of the prophecies in Revelation have come to pass, they can still be used again at the Lord's discretion. So, the enemy does try to get people to take his "mark" because he's always looking for worship. The physical "mark" may change over time again and again, but the point is that the devil is trying to get people to worship him in their hearts. The mark on the hand indicates what people do, and the mark on the forehead indicates how people think. In all things, we must be submitted to Jesus.

CHAPTER 9

THE BOWLS OF WRATH

A s we go through the things in Revelation that have happened, we have to keep in mind that John records successive visions, not necessarily successive events. In other words, the visions are not in chronological order. There are events that overlap, and there are even the same events recorded from different perspectives.

The bowl (vials) of the wrath of God are very similar to the trumpets and in fact, somewhat overlap the trumpets. Unlike the trumpets, however, the Bible records that the people on whom the bowl judgments are poured out do not repent, but instead curse God, similarly to the plagues in Egypt. So, this is something else to keep in mind as we go over these bowls of wrath.

The bowl judgments are often called "plagues" in English. This is the word "plege" (pronounced play-gay) in Greek. In English "plague" means disease or affliction, but in Greek, "plege" means: a blow, stripe, a wound; a public calamity, heavy affliction, plague. For example, in Luke 10:30 Jesus describes a man who fell among robbers, **"and they stripped him and beat (plege) him, and went away leaving him half dead."** Obviously, the man didn't receive a plague in the sense we would use the word in English. Instead, he was beaten, or received blows, wounds, or afflictions.

The bowls of wrath, or plagues, in Revelation 16 are similarly not really plagues, but they are afflictive judgments from the Lord Jesus Christ on those who do wickedly and who buy into the world system, which is also the beast system. These bowls of wrath are poured out over time; they are not short instances in history.

First Bowl (476-1453 AD – Decline and fall of the Roman Empire)

So the first went and poured out his bowl upon the earth, and a foul and loathsome sore came upon the men who had the mark of the beast and those who worshiped his image. (Revelation 16:2)

The first bowl is the period of time in which the Roman Empire fell. As we saw with the seals, Rome was plagued with civil wars, emperors rising and falling, and outside wars from the Goths, Huns, and Turks. These "soars" of affliction eventually led to the downfall of the Roman Empire. However, the downfall itself came in the second bowl of wrath.

Second & Third Bowls (1543-1923 AD Ottoman Empire Rise and Decline)

Then the second angel poured out his bowl on the sea, and it became blood as of a dead man; and every living creature in the sea died. Then the third angel poured out his bowl on the rivers and springs of water, and they became blood. And I heard the angel of the waters saying: "You are righteous, O Lord, The One who is and who was and who is to be, Because You have judged these things. For they have shed the blood of saints and prophets, And You have given them blood to drink. For it is their just due." (Revelation 16:4-6)

The second and third bowls of wrath are linked together. The second bowl depicts death on a mass scale in a large area – the sea. This was when the Ottoman Empire took over. They came first by sea, and overthrew what was left of the Roman Empire and the government that was adhering to Roman Catholicism. The second bowl of wrath was the final fall of the Roman Empire through the conquering of

Constantinople in 1543. The Ottoman Empire then spread and took over more land than the Romans had ever conquered.

The third bowl depicts the same type of judgment expanding out further – the rivers and springs. The third bowl – the wrath on the rivers and springs – was the continued expansion of the Ottoman Empire, which became bigger than the Roman Empire had ever been. Picture this expansion as moving up the rivers and into the springs of water as they sailed up the rivers, conquering and leaving blood in their wake. Death spread out from the sea to the rivers and springs of water through the Ottoman Empire.

These bowls are poured out against the Roman Catholic Church, which has set up a man who claims to be our "Father" on earth, claims to be Christ on earth, and claims to be "the source and guarantor of the Church's unity." (See The Pope: Christ on Earth - UA&P Universitas (uap.asia)) In other words, the Pope is taking the place of the Father, the Son, and the work of the Holy Spirit on earth. Sounds like an antichrist spirit, which it is.

We discussed how the Jesuits gained power in the Roman Catholic Church starting in 1540. They use their influence to back up the pope as they seek to take over all the nations of the world and bring them into submission to their one world order. Through their influence, in concert with the leadership of the Roman Catholic Church, there have been untold number of deaths and destruction over the centuries.

Because the spirit behind Catholicism is an antichrist spirit, the judgment of the Lord is against it. We need to keep in mind that this is a judgment against the government of the Roman Catholic Church, not the adherents to it. The people themselves mostly have no idea what is going on.

Here are a few examples to give you an idea of why judgment would come to the government of the Roman Catholic Church, and in so doing, to the Jesuit Order:

1209 – During the Albigensian Crusades in southern France, Roman Catholic crusaders slaughtered approximately 20,000 citizens of Beziers, France on July 22, 1209. By the time the Roman Catholic armies finished their crusade, almost the entire population of southern France (mostly Albigensian Christians) were exterminated (reference Massacre at Béziers -Wikipedia and www.executed   today.com/2009/07/22/1209-albigensian-crusade-cathars-beziers).

1481 – At the direction of the Roman Catholic inquisitors, authorities tortured, burned and slaughtered tens, even hundreds of thousands of people during the Spanish Inquisition (Jean Antoine Llorentine, History of the Inquistion; as cited in R.W. Thompson, The Papacy and the Civil Power {New York, 1876}; as cited in Dave Hunt, A Woman Rides the Beast).

1618-1648 – The Thirty Years War. This bloody, religious war was planned, instigated, and orchestrated by the Roman Catholic Jesuit order and its agents in an attempt to exterminate all the Protestants in Europe. Many countries in central Europe lost up to half their population (see Cushing B. Hassell, History of the Church of God, Chapter XVII).

1641-1649 - Eight years of Jesuit-instigated Roman Catholic murdering of Irish Protestants claims the lives of hundreds of thousands of Protestants (see Cushing B. Hassell, History of the Church of God, Chapter XVII).

By 1572 the Catholic Church held power in many European nations, especially France. This was the year of the St. Bartholomew's Day

Massacre in which the Catholics murdered a reported 10,000 people (men, women, and children) within a few days and continued the massacre over a period of three months until reportedly around 30,000 people were left dead. (See www.thoughtco.com/ saint-barthomomews-day-massacre-4173411 for more information.) Those who did not bow to Catholicism were killed.

Obviously, Nero Caesar was no longer alive, but the beast system was still active through the Catholic/Jesuit rule. Because of this evil, the second and third bowls of wrath came against the Roman Empire and the Catholic Church.

Bowls two and three were against the antichrist, beast system that is in the Roman Catholic/Jesuit Church. Wherever the Ottoman Empire spread, the Roman Catholic Church was kicked out.

Fourth Bowl (Napoleonic Wars 1799-1815 AD)

Then the fourth angel poured out his bowl on the sun, and power was given to him to scorch men with fire. And men were scorched with great heat, and they blasphemed the name of God who has power over these plagues; and they did not repent and give Him glory. (Revelation 16:8-9)

The Holy Roman Empire is different from the Roman Empire. It is the empire that was overtly run by the Roman Catholic Church, and the Jesuits in the background. It is recorded that Charlemagne or "Charles the Great" established it in 800 AD. Unlike other empires, the Holy Roman Empire was more of a collection of nations ruled by the Roman Catholic Church, who had authority to name the emperor. Enter in Napoleon Bonaparte.

The fourth bowl of wrath represents the Napoleonic wars, with Napoleon representing the sun. It only took Napoleon around eight years to scorch every kingdom in Europe, and to remove power from the Roman Catholic Church. He did this through conquering papal states, (areas governed overtly by the Roman Catholic Church), and by making himself more powerful than the pope. He first removed Pope Pius VI, by imprisoning him. During his imprisonment, the pope died. Then when the Roman Catholic bishops elected a new pope (Pope Pius VII), Napoleon invited the new pope to his crowning ceremony in 1804. But instead of allowing the pope to place the emperor's crown on his head, (which would mean the pope had more authority than the emperor) Napoleon took the crown and placed it on his own head, indicating his authority over the pope.

Yet, as the Scripture states, "[T]hey did not repent and give Him glory" (Revelation 16:9).

Fifth Bowl – Catholic Church Government Plunged into Darkness (1815-1929 AD)

Then the fifth angel poured out his bowl on the throne of the beast, and his kingdom became full of darkness; and they gnawed their tongues because of the pain. They blasphemed the God of heaven because of their pains and their sores, and did not repent of their deeds. (Revelation 16:10-11)

Following the fall of the Holy Roman Empire, the kingdom of the Beast was plunged into darkness. As we learned from the fourth bowl, the crowning of Napoleon as Emperor was the final straw in the fall of the Holy Roman Empire.

The fifth bowl of wrath was poured out on the "seat of the beast" as the Roman Catholic Church lost power, and finally lost all of their papal states when the last ones were annexed to Italy in 1870. From this point until 1929, the popes really had no land of their own.

But again, they **"did not repent of their deeds"** (Revelation 16:11).

Sixth Bowl (1700's – 1922 AD – Slow fall of the Ottoman Empire)

Then the sixth angel poured out his bowl on the great river Euphrates, and its water was dried up, so that the way of the kings from the east might be prepared. And I saw three unclean spirits like frogs coming out of the mouth of the dragon, out of the mouth of the beast, and out of the mouth of the false prophet. For they are spirits of demons, performing signs, which go out to the kings of the earth and of the whole world, to gather them to the battle of that great day of God Almighty. "Behold I am coming as a thief. Blessed is he who watches, and keeps his garments, lest he walk naked and they see his shame." And they gathered them together to the place in Hebrew, Armageddon. (Revelation 16:12-16)

The sixth bowl of wrath was a judgment that dried up the Ottoman Empire (the people {*river*} of the *Euphrates* who had been released during the 6th Trumpet and were used during the second and third bowls of wrath). The Byzantine Empire (Eastern Roman Empire) fell to the Turks in 1453. At its peak in the 1500's, the Ottoman Empire included Asia Minor; much of southeastern Europe, including Hungary, the Balkan Region, Greece, and parts of the Ukraine; the Middle East, including Iraq, Syria, Israel, and Egypt; North Africa; and parts of the Arabian Peninsula.

During the 18th and 19th centuries, the Ottoman Empire lost control of the Middle East, including losing Palestine to General Allenby of Great Britain in 1917 AD. The Ottoman Empire lasted for 600 years, but ultimately ended after a slow demise in 1922. What remains is now the modern nation of Turkey.

The fall of the Ottoman Empire overtime has allowed the way to be made for Communism, Socialism, and Satanism to join forces in an attempt to take over the world. And as the prophets have declared, this is the time of God's Great Reset, where He is doing a new thing in the earth. He is bringing justice and establishing righteousness. He is removing tares and pouring out His Spirit. Communism, Socialism, and Satanism will not prevail. Praise God!

Seventh Bowl (Current Judgment on the Beast System of Babylon)

> **Then the seventh angel poured out his bowl into the air, and a loud voice came out of the temple of heaven, from the throne, saying, "It is done!" And there were noises and thunderings and lightnings; and there was a great earthquake, such a mighty and great earthquake as had not occurred since men were on the earth. Now the great city was divided into three parts, and the cities of the nations fell. And great Babylon was remembered before God, to give her the cup of the wine of the fierceness of His wrath. Then every island fled away, and the mountains were not found. And great hail from heaven fell upon men, each hailstone about the weight of a talent. Men blasphemed God because of the plague of the hail, since that plague was exceedingly great.** (Revelation 16:17-21)

In the seventh bowl of wrath, an earthquake splits the great city into three parts. This is where we are. The Lord told us to imagine the seven mountains of influence in the world becoming three. An earthquake splitting the great city (Babylon) into three parts is what the Lord is talking about here. The following is a prophetic word regarding this very topic.

> *The Lord says: "I'm doing something different on the earth, as I've said before. Don't look at history to find the old patterns and ways. I'm doing something different! You have not come this way before, and this change is a global change. It will affect the entire planet in ways never before seen. I AM has given clues to the Prophets regarding the changes that will take place, but these clues are only clues and generalities. The extent and what all the countries and nations will look like in the future has*

104

not been imagined by man yet. The changes are of a magnitude that would impress Noah!

Imagine the 7 mountains of influence reduced to 3. What might those 3 remaining mountains be? What could take away the influence of these mountains? Prophet, tell the people to be ready to change their thinking in ways that will bring forth a new freedom that has never been seen before!

Imagine the freedom to be righteous and act righteously toward everyone, and expect the same from others! This is normal, say I AM, and it will be the NEW normal. Do not expect the old system with a makeover. The old system is headed to the trash heap. It's over and done!

Think about religion thrown out in the trash heap, too. All of its ways, rules, and ideas - all thrown out! That church with all of its earthly ideas, rules for holiness, places where men claimed to represent Me but never did... I AM spewing it out of My mouth. The stench in My nostrils was awful, but the taste is worse!

I Am trying to get <u>you</u> to dream with Me! Get rid of the lament, and the belief that your brothers and sisters are basically bad! Those who are filled with My Spirit are bad? Skepticism and mistrust are NOT virtues! Faith and trust are from Me. Don't believe the evil one anymore! Come, dream with Me! I Am Good! I Am the way, and I Am the truth, and I Am the life. Come!" (*Dare to Dream with God* – March 24, 2023)

When I dreamed about this, I saw three mountains. They were: Family, Government, and Commerce (Business). Entertainment, Media, Religion, and Education were no longer ruling. Instead, I saw the Holy Spirit ruling from the three mountains of Family, Government, and Commerce (business, work, etc.)

I saw Jesus ruling every mountain from top to bottom and from bottom to top. Who makes the education decisions? The family (parents) via the Holy Spirit. Who governs? The people under the direction of the Holy Spirit. Lastly, work will be honorable again. People will enjoy their work and do it well, instead of despising it and trying to get out of it. They'll take "pride" in it. *("My people's calling card will be their devotion to Me, their work ethic, and their generosity [love],"* the Lord said in a previous prophecy.)

It's going to be amazing, but right now we are in a time of great shaking. All who subscribe to the Beast System, or to Babylon will be judged. None will escape this judgment. These Communists, Socialists, and Satanists have infiltrated all of society with their control and Luciferian agenda. They've killed all who've stood in their way. But that world system, that Luciferian regime, has been under judgment. This includes the Deep State; the Globalist Elites, like those running the WEF; it includes the Jesuits and all of their front organizations; it includes the Roman Catholic Church (though certainly not all of the people in the church); and it includes the 13 or so families who pull the strings behind all of this. It includes the stench of Communism and Socialism. And it includes judgment against Satan himself and his kingdom of death and destruction.

We've mentioned that the people caught up in Roman Catholicism are not necessarily the ones under the seventh bowl of wrath, but those behind Roman Catholicism are. If you need convincing of some of the evil still being perpetrated by this church, here are a few modern examples:

1941 - 1945 - The Roman Catholic Ustashi in Yugoslavia butchered Hundreds of thousands of Yugoslav citizens, Serbs, Jews and Roma. And hundreds of thousands were forced to convert to Catholicism. (The Role of the Catholic Church in

Yugoslavia's Holocaust (fantompowa.net), Time to confront Croatia's hidden Holocaust - The Jerusalem Post (jpost.com))

1949 - 1953 - With the support from the Columbian government, the Roman Catholic Church had 60,000 Protestants and non-Catholics shot, drowned and emasculated. Pope Pius XII awarded the Columbian President with one of the highest awards the church can give.

You can also do a quick search for the history of sexual abuse in the Roman Catholic Church. Here's just one link: A history of priest sex abuse in the Catholic Church | khou.com.

Remember that the beast from the sea with the number 666 was Nero Caesar. The beast from the land is the pope. What this means is that over time, the Emperors of Rome worked with the popes. The popes crowned the emperors and basically shared power until the empire was destroyed, but still the popes held power in the world.

We will witness the downfall of the Roman Catholic Church in the 7th bowl of wrath. Emperor Nero operated in an antichrist spirit, as does each pope. The pope is supposedly Jesus on earth. That's blasphemy. It's just what Jesus prophesied, **"For many will come in My name, saying, 'I am the Christ,' and will deceive many"** (Matthew 24:5). This is what each pope does. They come in the name of Christ, declaring to be Christ on earth and deceive many. The Jesuits also come in the name of Christ, backing up the pope, and deceive many as they attempt to take over the world. Jesus will not stand for this.

Psalm 2:9 prophesies about Jesus: **"You shall break them with a rod of iron; You shall dash them to pieces like a potter's vessel."** And Jesus says this rod of iron will be in the hands of His overcoming church through His Apostles who wield the iron scepter. **"And he who overcomes, and keeps My works until the end, to him I will give** power over the nations – 'He shall rule them with a rod of iron; They shall be dashed to pieces like the potter's vessel…'". (Revelation 2:26-27)

And so, after this time of justice, the true church will arise, filled with the Holy Spirit, lives laid down to Jesus, and will establish Jesus as Lord in all the mountains of the earth. And those seven mountains will be reduced to three. And the earth will be filled with the knowledge of the glory of the Lord! (Habakkuk 2:14)

CHAPTER 10

THE END OF THE BABYLON WORLD SYSTEM

B abylon, also called the great city, is the world's system. Behind this system is the devil, and those who follow him: the Cabal, the Deep State, the Jesuits, the Luciferians, those who enforce Communism and Socialism. They are all the same. They worship the devil, and they have infiltrated all seven mountains of influence in every nation of the world. We are living in the end times when the Lord has prophesied through His prophets that He is doing a Great Reset in which He is destroying the world system. His judgment is coming upon those who do evil.

In Revelation 14, we saw that the great harvest begins even as the world system is being judged. The maturing of the tares is happening with the maturing of the wheat as the difference between those who are in Christ and those who are of the world is becoming more and more stark. This is what Jesus taught in the Parable of the Wheat and the Tares. We are actually in this time right now. Those of the world will mourn the destruction of the world system. Those of us in Christ will rejoice over it!

The enemy and those aligned with him have an evil agenda of steal, kill, destroy. This agenda comprises the Beast System that the woman rides on in Revelation 17.

> And I saw a woman sitting on a scarlet beast which was full of names of blasphemy, having seven heads and ten horns. The woman was arrayed in purple and scarlet, and adorned with gold and precious stones and pearls, having in her hand a golden cup

full of abominations and the filthiness of her fornication. And on her forehead a name was written: MYSTERY, BABYLON THE GREAT, THE MOTHER OF HARLOTS AND OF THE ABOMINATIONS OF THE EARTH. I saw the woman, drunk with the blood of the saints and with the blood of the martyrs of Jesus. And when I saw her, I marveled with great amazement. (Revelation 17:3b-6)

The woman is called "Babylon" in Revelation 18.

After these things I saw another angel coming down from heaven, having great authority, and the earth was illuminated with his glory. And he cried mightily with a loud voice, saying, "Babylon the great is fallen, is fallen, and has become a dwelling place of demons, a prison for every foul spirit, and a cage for every unclean and hated bird! For all the nations have drunk of the wine of the wrath of her fornication, the kings of the earth have committed fornication with her, and the merchants of the earth have become rich through the abundance of her luxury." (Revelation 18:1-3)

Babylon - the world system, or the beast system - has risen and fallen throughout history. We are again at that point where the enemy, through this system, and the Luciferians who have sold out to the devil, have poised themselves to take over the world. There will be people who mourn as the merchants and traders do in Revelation 18, but the saints shall rejoice, for they will inherit the land!

The Lord has prophesied that He's doing a Great Reset, and that evil will never rise to this level again. He's prophesied a devolution of technology, where instead of AI taking over, as the devil planned in his great reset, the Lord is going to walk back technology. The medical industry will be a shell of its former self. Our water and food will no longer be poisoned, and the seven mountains of influence will be reduced to three again.

The Lord has prophesied extensively about His Trumpet, and how he will lead the nations of the world in meting out justice, overseeing the new economic system, and bringing the nations into a time of freedom, prosperity, and goodness.

What we're living in and will witness is so much greater than the fall of the Roman Empire or the Ottoman Empire, or any other historical empire. This is truly the fall of the beast system on a level never before seen.

In Matthew 13:24-30, 36-43, Jesus tells the parable of the wheat and the tares. He says that the wheat and tares grow up together, but at the end of the age, the angels come and take out the tares and burn them. The following prophetic word was given on April 15, 2022 regarding the Parable of the Wheat and the Tares.

> *This is what the end of the age will look like because God has spoken this parable, and also its interpretation. Pay attention to this then. It is according to Jesus how it <u>will</u> be at the end of the age. This parable and its interpretation form a baseline for what the end of the age will look like.*
>
> *Take note that Jesus says specifically that the wheat should not be gathered before the tares, and specifically <u>does</u> say that the tares should be gathered by the angels at the end of the age, <u>then</u> the wheat. Other Scriptures regarding "the end of the age" or Jesus' second coming <u>will</u> agree with this. If it is interpreted differently, or a doctrine is formed in opposition to what Jesus <u>clearly</u> taught, it is wrong.*

Knowing that the angels will be gathering tares at the end of the age, we should be able to see the judgments in the Revelation of Jesus Christ as a separation of wheat and tares. The judgements poured out in Revelation are not scary to those of us in Christ. We know who we belong to. We know that we take shelter in the Most High. We know the wrath of God is not upon those of us in Christ. Therefore, the judgments of God are against the wicked. God's judgments are against those who become **"drunk with the blood of the saints and with the blood of the martyrs of Jesus."** (Revelation 17:6)

There is a clear separation throughout John's visions between the righteous and the wicked. The angels are clearly separating the tares from the wheat and throwing the tares into the fire to be burned. As one angel proclaimed, **"Therefore her plagues will come in one day – death and mourning and famine. And she will be utterly burned with fire, for strong is the Lord God who judges her"** (Revelation 18:8).

A separation has been happening since John's vision, but it grows more and more concise as the time of the end of the age grows nearer. We are now in the time when the Lord has said,

> *"I'm doing something different on the earth, as I've said before. Don't look at history to find the old patterns and ways. I'm doing something different! You have not come this way before, and this change is a global change. It will affect the entire planet in ways never before seen. I AM has given clues to the Prophets regarding the changes that will take place, but these clues are only clues and generalities. The extent and what all the countries and nations will look like in the future has not been imagined by man yet. The changes are of a magnitude that would impress Noah!"* (*Dare to Dream with God Prophecy* – March 24, 2023)

The angels are gathering tares. Jesus will have His bride pure in every respect, and the Lord will have His Great Reset.

Revelation 14, 17 and 18 depict the fall of Babylon, the beastly world system, and then in Revelation 19, Heaven is rejoicing. Even as the world system falls, the Bride of Christ is purified and made ready for her Groom.

After these things I heard a loud voice of a great multitude in heaven, saying, "Alleluia! Salvation and glory and honor and power belong to the Lord our God! For true and righteous are His judgments, because He has judged the great harlot who corrupted the earth with her fornications; and He has avenged on her the blood of His servants shed by her." Again they said, "Alleluia! Her smoke rises up forever and ever!" And the twenty-four elders and the four living creatures fell down and worshiped God who sat on the throne, saying, "Amen! Alleluia!" (Revelation 19:1-4)

Then John describes a vision of Jesus as the Conqueror, judgment on the wicked, and the beast and false prophet thrown into the lake of fire. The rest are killed with the sword that comes from the mouth of the Lord.

Now I saw heaven opened, and behold, a white horse. And He who sat on him was called Faithful and True, and in righteousness He judges and makes war. His eyes were like a flame of fire, and on His head were many crowns. He had a name written that no one knew except Himself. He was clothed with a robe dipped in blood, and His name is called The Word of God. And the armies in heaven, clothed in fine linen, white and clean, followed Him on white horses. Now out of His mouth goes a sharp sword, that with it He should strike the nations. And He Himself will rule them with a rod of iron. He Himself treads the winepress of the fierceness and wrath of the Almighty God. And He has on His robe and on His thigh a name written: KING OF KINGS AND LORD OF LORDS … And I saw the beast, the kings of the earth, and their armies, gathered together to make war against Him who sat on the horse and against His army. Then the beast was captured, and with him the false prophet who worked signs in his presence, by which he deceived those who received the mark of the beast and those who worshiped his image. These two were cast alive into the lake of fire burning with brimstone. And the rest were killed with the sword which proceeded from the mouth of Him who sat on the horse. And all the birds were filled with their flesh. (Revelation 19:11-16, 19-21)

This is imagery. There is not a literal army on earth that will fight the Lord and His army from heaven. It wouldn't even be a battle. One of God's angels could take out a whole army. There's also not a physical sword that proceeds from Jesus' mouth. Jesus is the word of God and He divides soul and spirit, joints and marrow. He judges the thoughts and intents of the heart. What John is seeing is a depiction of that judgment. The Word of God judges us.

The Lamb who was slain from the foundation of the world has been found worthy to judge – to open the scroll and its seals, as we read in Revelation 5. This scroll is a judgment of victory. No one was found worthy to open this judgment of victory until Jesus offered Himself on behalf of mankind. As such, He is the only One who is worthy to judge. It's He who determines who rules with a rod of iron, who is condemned to the lake of fire, and who is worthy to come to the marriage supper. He is King of kings and Lord of lords. The book of Revelation is the Revelation of Jesus Christ. It's all about Him, His worthiness, His justice, His power, His authority, and His love.

The Lord's narrative for this can be found prophesied in Habakkuk 2:12-14,

> Woe to him who builds a town with bloodshed,
> Who establishes a city by iniquity!
> Behold, is it not of the LORD of hosts
> That the peoples labor to feed the fire,
> And nations weary themselves in vain?
> For the earth will be filled
> With the knowledge of the glory of the LORD,

As the waters cover the sea.

The knowledge of the glory of the LORD will fill the earth! Jesus is the glory of God. Halleluiah, Jesus!

CHAPTER 11

THE TWO WITNESSES

T he two witnesses John saw in Revelation 11 help to pour out the knowledge of the glory of the Lord, of which Habakkuk prophesied. These two witnesses are the same anointed ones Zechariah prophesied about:

> I said, "I am looking, and there is a lampstand of solid gold with a bowl on top of it, and on the stand seven lamps with seven pipes to the seven lamps. Two olive trees are by it, one at the right of the bowl and the other at its left." … Then I answered and said to him, "What are these two olive trees – at the right of the lampstand and at its left?" And I further answered and said to him, "What are these two olive branches that drip into the receptacles of the two gold pipes from which the golden oil drains?" … So he said, "These are the two anointed ones, who stand beside the Lord of the whole earth." (Zechariah 4:2b-3, 11-12, 14)

Many years after Zechariah had his vision, the Apostle John also had a vision of the same anointed ones. The Lord said to John,

> "And I will give power to My two witnesses, and they will prophesy one thousand two hundred and sixty days, clothed in sackcloth." These are the two olive trees and the two lampstands standing before the God of the earth. And if anyone wants to harm them, fire proceeds from their mouth and devours their enemies. And if anyone wants to harm them, he must be killed in this manner. These have power to shut heaven, so that no rain falls in the days of their prophecy; and they have power over waters to

turn them to blood, and to strike the earth with all plagues, as often as they desire. When they finish their testimony, the beast that ascends out of the bottomless pit will make war against them, overcome them, and kill them. And their dead bodies will lie in the street of the great city which spiritually is called Sodom and Egypt, where also our Lord was crucified. Then those from the peoples, tribes, tongues, and nations will see their dead bodies three-and-a-half days, and not allow their dead bodies to be put in graves. And those who dwell on the earth will rejoice over them, make merry, and send gifts to one another, because these two prophets tormented those who dwell on the earth. Now after the three-and-a-half days the breath of life from God entered them, and they stood on their feet, and great fear fell on those who saw them. And they heard a loud voice from heaven saying to them, "Come up here." ... Then the seventh angel sounded: And there were loud voices in heaven, saying, "The kingdoms of this world have become the kingdoms of our Lord and of His Christ, and He shall reign forever and ever!" (Revelation 11:3-12a, 15)

These two anointed ones are the apostles and prophets who are submitted to Jesus and learn from Him. John saw the prophets and apostles from the beginning of time until the death of the first-generation apostles. This would include Enoch, Abraham, David, Moses, Isaiah, Ezekiel, Elijah, John the Baptist and all the other prophets, as well as the apostles of the New Covenant. These apostles and prophets brought the witness of Jesus Christ. They poured out the golden oil, which is the pure word of the Lord, or the testimony of Jesus through His Spirit. They came with signs and wonders. Fire came down from heaven on those who wanted to hurt Elijah. Moses turned water to blood and called for plagues. Elijah called for no rain, and it didn't rain until he prayed again for rain. Ananias and Saphira dropped dead at a word from Apostle Peter, and so much more.

After the first-generation church with their apostles and prophets, there is very minimal heard about apostles and prophets until recently. The beast, which was at first Nero and then the same antichrist spirit in other Roman Emperors sought to destroy the witnesses of the Lord. Later, the Roman Catholic Church took over "Christianity" and got rid of those they didn't want, which would be the Lord Jesus' chosen ministers. Even after the Reformation, the Institutional Church would not allow apostles and prophets to minister. The apostles and prophets chosen by Christ went about the earth unknown and persecuted; to all the world, they were dead. The beast had overcome them, and they've lain dead for those of the world system to gloat over since then.

However, since the coming of the Lord's Trumpet and the beginning of the Justice of the Lord and His Great Reset, the prophets have risen up from all over the world. The Lord has resurrected His prophets, breathing life into them. They've been given a voice and a platform. They are still persecuted, but they are being listened to and fear is coming on the evil ones who hear them. Why do you think they kick the prophets and apostles off social media and try to silence them? Why do the prophets and apostles get attacked all the time? Their enemies are afraid. Those who see the resurrection of the witnesses are terrified.

After this time of the prophets, the time of the apostles will come again. In fact, it is upon us even as we write this book. The Lord is breathing life into His two witnesses and causing them to stand on their feet. The apostles and prophets are called to ascend spiritually to their place in heaven where they stand next to the Lord of all the earth, bringing to the church what they see and hear. They witness of the Lord Jesus Christ! Through their brokenness and suffering, they are counted worthy to pour out the golden oil of the testimony of Jesus.

John heard, "Come up here," and he went in the Spirit. Kirk frequently hears, "Come up here," and he brings back what he has seen and heard. Other prophets and apostles do the same. The ones who submit to being taught by the LORD are the ones He gives of Himself to. When Jesus called the first 12 to be apostles, He called them to be "with Him." He gave of Himself to them. It is the same today. He calls His witnesses to be with Him. These are the apostles and prophets who will witness of Jesus.

In a vison, I (Kirk) was taken to a place, and I saw the Lord of All sitting on a lone throne. His hair was white. His eyes were a flame of fire alternating to normal brown eyes, like between wrath and love. He did not look old, but vigorous and strong. In His right hand He held an iron scepter. It had a handle at the bottom and a cross at the top. On His left stood the archangel Gabriel, and on His right stood the archangel Michael. The very air was charged with power, and there was a rather serious tone. The Lord Jesus sat as a statue holding the scepter.

Then when the time was right, He spoke. Lightning flashed in all directions from the throne, followed by thick smoke rolling behind the lightning. The whole place was filled with smoke. I did not understand what He said, but as I watched, two people solemnly walked up to the throne before the Lord of All.

These two represented the Apostles and the Prophets. As they approached, simultaneously they knelt on one knee before the Lord. They stayed this way for a short time. The Lord rose up from His throne and stood before them. Gabriel and Michael stepped forward and stood on the sides of the two who knelt, as if to steady them. The two kneeling faced the Lord. The angels and the Lord faced the Apostle and Prophet.

The Lord raised the iron scepter, holding it in both hands by the handle and laid it first on the Apostle's head. As He lifted it back up, a flame of fire was burning on, or perhaps above, the Apostle's head. He then stepped to the side of the Prophet, and Gabriel also stepped to the side of the Prophet. Fire was also left on the Prophet's head.

The Lord and the angels then stepped back, and the Lord again sat down and spoke. The lightning and smoke rolled out from Him, and the power of Him charged the room! I could not understand what He said because of the thunder. The Apostle and Prophet then stood to their feet, looked at the Lord for a few seconds and then turned around and walked forward, away from the throne. The flames of fire on their heads remained on them as they walked. Amen. (Vision of Jesus with Iron Scepter, Fire, & Two Witnesses – July 28, 2023)

In Revelation 10, a mighty angel cries with a loud voice and when he does, the seven thunders sound their voices. John was told to seal up what they had spoken. Then the angel declares that in days of the sounding of the seventh angel, when he is about to sound, the mystery of God would be finished, as He declared to His servants the prophets.

Enter Revelation 11 with the two witnesses. After they are raised from the dead, the seventh angel sounds, and that is when the voices in heaven (where the two witnesses are spiritually standing) say, "The kingdoms of this world have become the kingdoms of our Lord and of His Christ, and He shall reign forever and ever!" Then the elders worship God saying the time of His wrath has come, His judgment (recompense to the wicked and the righteous) has come, and that He will destroy those who destroy the earth.

All of this is exactly like what the Lord has been prophesying for several years now. He's judging the wicked, including those who've destroyed the earth by poisoning the water, ground, plants, animals, and people. He's bringing His recompense to the wicked and the just. It will be very good for those of us who have stayed faithful to Him, and it will be very bad for those who have opposed Him. He has raised up the prophets and is raising up the apostles to lead the church and the earth into His Great Reset, into a time of plenty, into the millennial reign, where the seven mountains are taken over by righteousness and eventually reduced to three mountains of influence, where Jesus is the foundation.

The iron scepter is a scepter of judgment and righteousness. The Apostles and Prophets come to make things right. The fire is the purity and power of the Lord Himself. Jesus is coming for a pure bride without spot or wrinkle. The fire that proceeds from Him through His witnesses will purify His church. The Lord is once again giving of Himself to His Two Witnesses - those Apostles and Prophets who *only* seek the glory of the Lord.

The Lord has prophesied that the latter outpouring of the Holy Spirit would by far exceed the former outpouring. He said the last will be first and the first will be last. He has said the mighty acts done by the first apostles would look like child's play in these last days. He has warned the church that they would need to respect His Spirit and His ministers, especially His apostles. The whole world is going to gasp when these two stand to their feet! Satan has tried to keep these witnesses buried for over 2,000 years. But they stand up on their feet! And they stand next to the Lord of all the earth pouring out the golden oil of the pure word of His Spirit. (Zechariah 4)

He is beginning to set the Apostles and Prophets on fire, and the world will never be the same. Jesus has prophesied that the Latter Rain of the Holy Spirit will be much greater than the former. His ministers will walk in authority and power like the world has never seen, and none more than His apostles. Their cry will be, **"The kingdoms of this world have become the kingdoms of our Lord and of His Christ, and He shall reign forever and ever!"** (Revelation 11:15)

CHAPTER 12

THE MILLENNIAL REIGN & THE NEW JERUSALEM

———————— ◆ ◂◂ ◆ ▸▸ ◆ ————————

Revelation 20:1-6 reads,

> Then I saw an angel coming down from heaven, having the key to the bottomless pit and a great chain in his hand. He laid hold of the dragon, that serpent of old, who is the Devil and Satan, and bound him for a thousand years; and he cast him into the bottomless pit, and shut him up, and set a seal on him, so that he should deceive the nations no more till the thousand years were finished. But after these things he must be released for a little while. And I saw thrones, and they sat on them, and judgment was committed to them. Then I saw the souls of those who had been beheaded for their witness to Jesus and for the word of God, who had not worshiped the beast or his image, and had not received his mark on their foreheads or on their hands. And they lived and reigned with Christ for a thousand years. But the rest of the dead did not live again until the thousand years were finished. This is the first resurrection. Blessed and holy is he who has part in the first resurrection. Over such the second death has no power, but they shall be priests of God and of Christ, and shall reign with Him a thousand years.

The Lord has said that evil will never rise to the level that it is at currently (*Trump Administers Justice Prophecy* – July 2, 2021). This is because the enemy will never have the resources that he has right now. Let's look at what will happen because of this.

There is currently a battle in the heavenlies between the angelic and the demonic. When the angels and demons fight, the LORD never loses, but instead the demonic gets destroyed, or is bound. In these end times, the demonic is getting bound for a time, and since the devil is head over the demonic, it is like he is bound.

The Lord is also exposing the lies of the enemy regarding authority. We, who are in Christ, have been given all authority in heaven and on earth. The enemy has lied to the church about this truth for a long time. But think about what will happen when the sons of God rise up in their authority. Who will be in charge? Will it be the globalist elites? The Luciferians? The Socialists? The devil? No. It will be those who are in Christ.

The Lord will have His Great Reset. He has prophesied that during His reset, the righteous are taking over, and the people will demand those who lead them to be of the Holy Spirit. The Lord has prophesied that people will act righteously and expect others to act righteously. This is normal, He's said. Since righteousness will abound and so much deception will be bound, it will be easier for people to come to the Lord. Hence, the Great Harvest and the ability to establish the Kingdom of Heaven on Earth. He's prophesied, long life, great health, prosperity, and goodness.

Think about what it will be like to have two billion youth, besides older people coming to the Lord as the tares are removed from the earth. What happens when someone is born again? They come from death to life, right? Doesn't the Scripture say that the dead will rise up and reign with Christ in these times? Remember that the things in the vision of the Revelation of Jesus Christ are not literal, but symbolic.

Yes, Jesus is physically coming back at some point, but He doesn't need to physically set up a kingdom in what is termed the Millennial

Reign. He rules through His people. They will bind the enemy using their authority. They will establish righteousness in the earth through His Spirit. They will disciple those being born again to actually follow the Holy Spirit and only live for Jesus.

The Lord says the prophecy found in Isaiah 43:19 (NASB)

applies to this time:

"Behold, I Am going to do something new. NOW it WILL spring up; will you not be aware of it? I will even make a roadway in the wilderness, rivers in the desert."

Yes, Prophet! Listen up! I Am doing a new thing! The Lord of Hosts, yes I even I, Adonai. I Am visiting a new thing upon the earth! It will be a NEW THING for which there is no precedent and <u>nothing</u> like it has been done before. Looking at the past while trying to envision the future is worthless. Have I not said a new thing?

This is a rescue mission, says the Lord! In My great Mercy, Love, and Patience, I Am going to intervene in the affairs of men once more. But the end is not yet.

I Am releasing My Holy Apostles after this time, and they shall only bow the knee to My Son, and only follow Him. My Apostles and Prophets shall build a church! This church shall be the one without spot or wrinkle and it shall be glorious in the depth of its faith in Him and in the revelation of the Christ! My Shekinah Glory shall once again be found on earth! I shall settle on a people, and their light shall shine into the darkness, and those outside of this light shall be drawn to it just as a moth is drawn to light. The stench shall be put out of My nostrils, says the Lord, and My people shall experience prosperity and favor, and they shall praise My Name. Amen" (*The Lord is Doing a New Thing Prophecy* – July 1, 2021).

Again, the Lord prophesies about this time using Hosea 3.

The Lord says, "Turn back to your countries and love them once again." In the USA, it will really be a government of the people, by the people, and FOR the people once again. In fact, we'll be nationalists in each country we are from.

As each country cleans up, we will each treat each other well again. Revival will sweep this nation, and the world. The criteria for leadership will <u>truly</u> be God first, not a false claim with no power. Just as in the account of Hosea and Israel, there will be an absence of government for a brief time in which the people will choose God, and the Trumpet will return. Just before Trump comes back, it will be the darkest of times for some people (those who mourn the fall of Babylon), but not for others (the righteous). As Hosea writes, **"They will come trembling to the Lord and to His blessings in the last days."** *(Hosea 3 Prophecy – July 23, 2022)*

These are only two prophetic words out of close to 200 given to us as of 2023. The Lord has continually prophesied about the judgment He is bringing on the wicked and the blessing that is coming to the righteous. The Lord has been prophesying about His Great Reset for some time. He says He's doing a new thing, and it's not something we've ever seen before. He says the earth will be changed forever, and He's even told us that the angels haven't been this excited since the birth of Christ.

Here are a few more excerpts of prophetic words to give you an idea of what to look forward to.

The Lord says: "I'm doing something different on the earth, as I've said before. Don't look at history to find the old patterns and ways. I'm doing something different! You have not come this way before, and this change is a global change. It will affect the entire planet in ways never before seen. I AM has given clues to the Prophets regarding the changes that will take place, but these clues are only clues and generalities. The extent and what all the countries and nations will look like in the future has not been imagined by man yet. The changes are of a magnitude that would impress Noah!" (Dare to Dream with God Prophecy – March 24, 2023)

"Now, My people, look to the future with great anticipation and joy! Your God is love and He is good! Can evil ever really win? Could Satan really challenge Me? It is said on the earth that this upheaval is not political or cultural, but that it is spiritual. In particular, it is good vs. evil. Or, maybe God vs. Satan. But I tell you, NO! This notion assumes that there is a chance that I AM could lose! There is no such chance. The chaos that you see is My love at work. It is a rescue mission that I AM undertaking in a sovereign manner. I AM inviting My saints to participate in this because I wish to revel in the great victory that they will have! We are using Plan A. There is no fallback plan, no secondary plan, such as Plan B. My plan is perfect and cannot fail.

The result of this great victory will change the earth forever. I have detailed these changes in other 'words' and prophecies. Amen." (Prophetic Update regarding DJT & God's Great Reset – December 30, 2022)

The Lord told Kirk to look up to Heaven in the Spirit; so he did. He saw the whole sky filled with angels. He couldn't see anything but angels. They were everywhere. The Lord said, "It has begun." Kirk asked what had begun, and the Lord answered that He's taking out the tares. (Vision from March 18, 2023)

As we read these prophecies and look at Scripture, we can see the Lord's plan unfolding for what is termed the "millennial reign." This millennial reign is not necessarily 1,000 years, but it is indicative of a long time. The word "thousand" used in Revelation 20 can mean thousand and can mean the "plural of an uncertain affinity." This time is an extended time, but it is not limited to 1,000 literal years.

Also, as stated, the Lord does not need to physically return for this reign to happen. Although, He will return a second time at some point. His return will be a sudden event and will indicate the final judgment. Nebuchadnezzar's dream of the statue shows how it will be.

> **"And in the days of these kings** (Roman Emperors) **the God of heaven will set up a kingdom which shall never be destroyed; and the kingdom shall not be left to other people; it shall break in pieces and consume all these kingdoms, and it shall stand forever. Inasmuch as you saw that the stone was cut out of the mountain without hands, and that it broke in pieces the iron, the bronze, the clay, the silver, and the gold – the great God has made known to the king what will come after this. The dream is certain, and its interpretation is sure."** (Daniel 2:44-45)

Jesus came to earth and set up a kingdom. This kingdom is not something where the king reigns and then when he dies, there's fighting for the kingdom – it **"shall not be left to other people."** It's a kingdom that shall never be destroyed. It's a kingdom that completely takes over, just like a mustard seed grows into the largest tree in the garden, or just like leaven works its way through the whole lump of dough. These parables Jesus taught show us that His kingdom will never end, and it will completely take over. During the "millennial" reign, the church of Jesus Christ will establish the kingdom of heaven on earth like never before.

We have been taught and have believed, and even taught at times, that there will be a resurrection of the physical dead in which the righteous are resurrected first. Then sometime later the wicked are resurrected. This is false. While there will be a physical resurrection of the dead, the first resurrection spoken of in Revelation 20 is now. In order to understand the resurrection of the dead, we have to first understand the resurrection of Jesus Christ.

Jesus is the first born from the dead. This means He is the first to rise from the dead who will never die again. We become partakers of everlasting life because He has been resurrected. The same Spirit that raised Him from the dead, lives in us who believe and will also raise us up from the dead. If Christ has not been raised from the dead, then we are still dead in our sins and there is no hope of eternal life for us. (See 1 Corinthians 15 for a great exposé on the death and resurrection of Jesus Christ.)

It was common knowledge that there will be a resurrection at the last day when Christ returns. Martha said to Jesus, **"I know that he [Lazarus] will rise again in the resurrection at the last day"** (John 11:24). Jesus did not dispute this because it was common knowledge among those who followed the Lord. All who have ever lived, will rise from the dead. Some will go to eternal life and some to eternal death.

> **Do not marvel at this; for the hour is coming in which all who are in the graves will hear His voice and come forth – those who have done good, to the resurrection of life, and those who have done evil, to the resurrection of condemnation.** (John 5:28-29)

When it is time for the "White Throne" judgment, the unrighteous are sent to the lake of burning fire, where they are tormented forever and ever. We who are in Christ live forever and ever because death cannot keep us. Christ mastered death and it has no hold on Him; therefore, if we are found to be in Him, death has no hold on us either.

> **Then I saw a great white throne and Him who sat on it, from whose face the earth and the heaven fled away. And there was found no place for them. And I saw the dead, small and great, standing before God, and books were opened. And another book**

was opened, which is the Book of Life. And the dead were judged according to their works, by the things which were written in the books. The sea gave up the dead who were in it, and Death and Hades delivered up the dead who were in them. And they were judged, each one according to his works. Then Death and Hades were cast into the lake of fire. This is the second death. And anyone not found written in the Book of Life was cast into the lake of fire. (Revelation 20:11-15)

The unrighteous die a second death, which has no power over the righteous. Romans 6:8-9 reads, **"Now if we died with Christ, we believe that we shall also live with Him, knowing that Christ, having been raised from the dead, dies no more. Death no longer has dominion over Him."** If we are in Christ, death no longer has dominion over us either and we will not die a second time. In fact, we won't really die a first time because our spirits will eternally live; whereas someone who dies outside of Christ will never eternally live, but instead will eternally die.

This is also why Jesus says in Matthew 5:29-30,

> "If your right eye causes you to sin, pluck it out and cast it from you; for it is more profitable for you that one of your members perish, than for your whole body to be cast into hell. And if your right hand causes you to sin, cut it off and cast it from you; for it is more profitable for you that one of your members perish, than for your whole body to be cast into hell."

Sin is so serious, it's better to suffer the loss of a limb than to be raised to life just to die the second death and have your whole body, soul, and spirit sent to hell. Of course, neither we, nor Jesus, are advocating for maiming yourself. The point was to show how serious it is to be led astray from the path of life.

Therefore, we need to keep our eyes on Jesus, and follow the Holy Spirit. First John 3:2 says, **"Beloved, now we are children of God; and it has not yet been revealed what we shall be, but we know that when He is revealed, we shall be like Him, for we shall see Him as he is."** The more we see Him now, the more we will be like Him now. **"As we have borne the image of the man of dust, we shall also bear the image of the heavenly Man"** (1 Corinthians 15:49). Whether we are awake or asleep, we will see Him as He is, and as we "see" Him, we bear His image.

Throughout the New Testament, those who die in Christ are referred to as sleeping, but those who die outside of Christ are considered dead. This is because death has no dominion over those in Christ, but those without Christ die and are raised up only to die again and suffer eternally in Hell.

> **For this we say to you by the word of the Lord, that we who are alive and remain until the coming of the Lord will by no means precede those who are asleep. For the Lord Himself will descend from heaven with a shout, with the voice of an archangel, and with the trumpet of God. And the dead in Christ will rise first. Then we who are alive and remain shall be caught up together with them in the clouds to meet the Lord in the air. And thus we shall always be with the Lord.** (1 Thessalonians 4:15-17)

Notice the word "asleep" above. Other examples include Jesus referring to Jairus' daughter as sleeping instead of dead. (Luke 8:52 – Children are saved until they are able to choose life or death.) Also, Jesus refers to Lazarus as sleeping (John 11:11), and Paul refers to those who died in Christ as sleeping (1 Corinthians 15:51). Whereas the widow of Nain's son was referred to as dead (Luke 7:11-17).

In the New Testament, the saved are always referred to as having fallen asleep when they die. Whereas the wicked are simply called dead when they die. This is because when a believer dies, they're not actually dead. You cannot kill someone in Christ. They are eternally alive.

Jesus says in Mark 12:26-27,

> **"But concerning the dead, that they rise, have you not read in the book of Moses, in the burning bush passage, how God spoke to him, saying, 'I am the God of Abraham, the God of Isaac, and the God of Jacob'? He is not the God of the dead, but of the living. You are therefore greatly mistaken."**

Those in Christ are not dead. **"So when this corruptible has put on incorruption, and this mortal has put on immortality, then shall be brought to pass the saying that is written: 'Death has been swallowed up in victory.'"** (1 Corinthians 15:54) Praise God!

The Lord has said that His angels are removing the tares and resurrecting the church. The true Church has for all intents and purposes been as though dead. Jesus is removing the institutional church and raising up a pure bride. Those in Christ will rise up during this time and take over the areas of influence in the world. They will join with the new believers who are being born again in the End Times Harvest. They will be in positions of authority on the earth because righteousness will prevail. The Lord says that His Apostles and Prophets will especially be raised up to positions of authority.

"In My Great Reset men won't desire things outside of Me like they do right now. They will desire Me and what comes from Me. This isn't something that will happen instantaneously. My fivefold will be very active in teaching My ways, how to follow My Spirit. They will be active in government, especially My Apostles and Prophets, because they will help to lay a right foundation in the governments of the nations of

the world." (What Causes Men to Sin & Five-Fold Active in Government Word – August 9, 2023)

With the tares removed, establishing righteousness will be a lot easier. And those who have not been taken out as tares in this Great Reset will have an opportunity to turn to the Lord.

Out of respect for the dead, history books will be rewritten with no mention of the names of those who have perpetrated the great wickedness we see right now. They have done horrendous atrocities that we barely know about. They have murdered children, they've started endless wars, killed people in purposeful famines, outright murdered those who opposed them, killed people through "medicine," and the list goes on. Out of respect for these people, the evil ones' names will be omitted from history books. This doesn't mean we won't remember history. It just means their desire to be remembered personally will not come to fruition because they were so incredibly evil.

Let's look at one more excerpt from a prophecy given in 2022.

In a very short time, the people will come out without fear. And the Cabal shall be in fear, hiding from the people and justice. Unlike the people's fears, those of the Cabal will come upon them! Yes, the very thing they have feared most; it will come upon them. They will have nowhere to hide. Even the secret places which they have taken great care to hide, and have been ruthless in doing so, have been, or will be, found out. Then they will be made to watch as their fortunes are removed from them. And after that comes the justice that is fitting for those who knew what they were doing, and getting into, who have left Me, and joined with Satan and his servants and cannot, even if they wanted to, come back to Me. The world will then learn the depth of the depravity it has been under. The history books shall be re-written and truth shall be told to those who desire to learn. But those liars and charlatans who have written all the lies, it shall be that their names shall be removed from every page, every computer, and nobody will even mention their names again out of respect for those who have lost their lives by the hands of these evil ones. Their desire to rule over the earth and their accomplishments erased! No one shall speak of them again. Their names shall be as the scum of the earth that no one wants to think about, says the Lord! Yes, and the years shall be known (as the prophet [Enlow] declared) 'Before Trump and After Trump.' Amen." (The Coming In and the Going Out Prophecy, February 1, 2022)

We are entering into the "Millennial Reign," and the Bride of Christ will be purified during this time.

Now I saw a new heaven and a new earth, for the first heaven and the first earth had passed away. Also there was no more sea. Then I, John, saw the holy city, New Jerusalem, coming down out of heaven from God, prepared as a bride adorned for her husband … Then one of the seven angels who had the seven bowls filled with the seven last plagues came to me saying, "Come, I will show you the bride; the Lamb's wife." And he carried me away in the Spirit to a great and high mountain, and showed me the city, the holy Jerusalem, descending out of heaven from God … Also she had a great and high wall with twelve gates, and twelve angels at the gates, and names written on them, which are the names of the twelves tribes of Israel … Now the wall of the city had twelve foundations, and on them were the names of the twelve apostles of the Lamb … The city is laid out as a square; its length is as great as its breadth. And he measured the city with the reed: twelve thousand furlongs. Its length, breadth, and height are equal ... But I saw no temple in it, for the Lord God Almighty and the Lamb are its temple … (Revelation 21:1-2, 9-10, 12, 14, 16, 22).

The Bride of Christ is depicted as the New Jerusalem, or the holy city, because the Bride of Christ is holy. Her foundation is right, for it's founded on the apostles and prophets. It's perfectly laid out, filled with gold and jewels because her Bridegroom has made her perfect and pure. The temple in the city is the Father and the Son, because the Bride has no other God. There are no idols in the true Church of Christ.

Ezekiel saw the New Jerusalem pictured as a perfectly proportioned cube as well, only he saw it as a temple. Similarly to John, Ezekiel saw his vision after Israel was miraculously resurrected (Valley of the Dry Bones), which John saw as the first resurrection. Then Ezekiel saw a final battle in which the enemy was completely destroyed, which John saw in Revelation 20. After these things, they both witnessed the Bride of Christ in her perfection. (See Ezekiel 37-47.)

The Scriptures indicating a pure bride will be fulfilled.

> **You are... fellow citizens with the saints and members of the household of God, having been built upon the foundation of the apostles and prophets, Jesus Christ Himself being the chief cornerstone, in whom the whole building, being fitted together, grows into a holy temple in the Lord, in whom you also are being built together for a dwelling place of God in the Spirit** (Ephesians 2:19-22).

We shall all be in unity in the faith and the knowledge of the Son of God. We shall be perfect, having attained to the measure of the fullness of Christ. We shall not be fooled by the enemy's trickery, but will be mature and complete, operating fully in love (Ephesians 4:11-16). The Lord has said that the Holy Spirit would never leave us or forsake us. We shall be filled with the Spirit of Christ, even in Heaven. The Lord shall sit enthroned on our hearts throughout eternity.

This is a picture of the New Jerusalem. It is a picture of the Bride of Christ. It is a revelation of the LORD Jesus Christ as He makes His Church like Him. Wow! Even so, come Lord Jesus!

CHAPTER 13

CAN GOD USE PROPHECIES MORE THAN ONCE?

All Scripture is given by inspiration of God, and is profitable for doctrine, for reproof, for correction, for instruction in righteousness... (2 Timothy 3:17)

When a vision, prophecy, or revelation is from God, then He's the One who gets to interpret what it means. We've all read the Scriptures and had the Holy Spirit speak to us through them at one time or another. In fact, this is a very common way that He speaks.

Take the Psalms for example. David wrote many of the Psalms, and yet even though they were true for David at the time, the Holy Spirit can use them today on a personal basis for each of us at various points in our lives.

Or take Isaiah 45. Isaiah was clearly prophesying about King Cyrus. And yet, the LORD has used the Cyrus prophecies to speak about President Donald J. Trump.

Or we've also seen that Nero Caesar was the beast with the number 666 assigned to him. And yet, the Holy Spirit has shown that the antichrist spirit with the beast system works through many people.

Even though many of the prophecies in Scripture have come to pass, even many regarding the end times, the Lord can use the same prophecies again at His discretion. This doesn't mean, however, that

He *must* use the prophecies again. It just means that we cannot put God in a box. He's able to do as He pleases.

With this in mind then, we do not have to look for the fulfilled prophecies about the end times to happen all over again. Daniel was told that the words were **"closed up and sealed till the time of the end"** by the angel who was explaining things to him (Daniel 12:9). Whereas John was told not to seal up the prophecy because the time was at hand (Revelation 22:10). In other words, Daniel wanted to know the end of these things, but couldn't. We, however, are in the end times when we can understand as the Holy Spirit reveals to us. And as He reveals what has happened, and what is happening, and what is yet to come, He is able to use a fulfilled prophecy to prophesy about something else. However, He does not have to, nor should we keep looking for fulfillment of something that He has revealed has already happened. If He wants to use a prophecy again, He will bring it to our attention, but we don't need to go digging for it.

In all things we submit to the Holy Spirit and what He reveals to us about Jesus. As Paul writes, **"Now we have received, not the spirit of the world, but the Spirit who is from God, that we might know the things that have been freely given to us by God"** (1 Corinthians 3:12).

As we enter into the End Times, consider what Isaiah prophesied:

> The word that Isaiah the son of Amoz saw concerning Judah and Jerusalem.
> Now it shall come to pass in the latter days
> *That* the mountain of the Lord's house
> Shall be established on the top of the mountains,
> And shall be exalted above the hills;
> And all nations shall flow to it.
> Many people shall come and say,
> "Come, and let us go up to the mountain of the Lord,

> To the house of the God of Jacob;
> He will teach us His ways,
> And we shall walk in His paths."
> For out of Zion shall go forth the law,
> And the word of the Lord from Jerusalem.
> He shall judge between the nations,
> And rebuke many people;
> They shall beat their swords into plowshares,
> And their spears into pruning hooks;
> Nation shall not lift up sword against nation,
> Neither shall they learn war anymore. (2:1-4)

This prophecy is applicable for today. The Lord is judging, Zion and Jerusalem represent the true church, and out of her will come the pure oil of the word of the Lord when the apostles and prophets are in their rightful place. Peace will reign, and there will not be fighting between nations as we see now. And the mountain of the Lord's house will be established on the tops of the mountains of influence in the world.

The fivefold will be governing the church, and many of them will have a role in the nations. Although, not every governing office in the nations will be run by someone of the fivefold. Others will govern in the nations too.

The world is entering the greatest times in history where the Holy Spirit is poured out like never before. Jesus will be lifted high as never before. And the church will walk in authority, power, love, and truth as never before.

The Holy Spirit has purposely not included all of the end times details in this book. The Lord desires us instead to have a big picture overview with some of the details in order that we may see things the way God sees them. Humility is to agree with God. When we get

His perspective and see things the way He sees them, He is able to pour His grace upon us because He gives grace to the humble.

Similarly to Esther, we have been born for such a time as this. We each have a role to play, we each have a unique calling, and we each are empowered by the Holy Spirit to make disciples of Jesus Christ. Therefore, keep Jesus as your focus, and in your hearts always lift Him up. He is truly King of kings and Lord of lords! Amen.

www.ingramcontent.com/pod-product-compliance
Lightning Source LLC
LaVergne TN
LVHW052029080426
835513LV00018B/2246